Growing Beyond Survival

This book was made possible through the generous support of the Department of Mental Health, Mental Retardation and Substance Abuse Services in the State of Maine and the New York State Office of Mental Health.

Growing Beyond Survival

A SELF-HELP TOOLKIT FOR MANAGING
TRAUMATIC STRESS

Elizabeth G. Vermilyea, M.A.

The Sidran Press
Baltimore, Maryland

This book is designed to provide information in regard to the subject matter covered. It is sold with the understanding that the publisher and the author are not engaged in providing psychological or professional services through this medium. If such professional advice or service is required, the services of a competent professional should be sought. The purpose of this workbook is to educate, inform and enlighten persons who wish to use self-help tools for self-understanding, or those who may be working with such individuals professionally. The author and Sidran Press will have neither liability nor responsibility to any person or entity with respect to any loss or damage caused, or alleged to be caused, directly or indirectly, by the information in this book.

Book and cover design by Kachergis Book Design, Pittsboro, North Carolina.

Printed in the United States of America

9 8 7 6 5   07 06 05

LIBRARY OF CONGRESS CATALOGING-IN-PUBLICATION DATA
Vermilyea, Elizabeth G., 1969–
    Growing beyond survival : a self-help toolkit for managing traumatic stress /
    Elizabeth G. Vermilyea.
        p.   cm.
    Includes bibliographical references.
    ISBN 1-886968-09-8 (pbk : alk.paper)
    1. Post-traumatic stress disorder—Popular works.   2. Self-help techniques.
    3. Psychic trauma.   I. Title.
RC552.P67 V47 2000
616.85'21—dc21
                                                                                    00-034445

Contents

Preface

Growing Beyond Survival is a self-help workbook. It is not meant to take the place of counseling or therapy. If you experience emotional or physical problems associated with traumatic experiences, it can be important to seek professional assistance. For information about resources in your area, you can contact The Sidran Traumatic Stress Foundation at 410-825-8888 or visit the website at www.sidran.org.

A Note from the Author:

A reader who reviewed this suggested that I put a note right in the front about why I wrote it. I decided to take her advice.

Years ago, when I first began working with survivors, someone showed me a book called *The Silver Boat,* by Ann Adams. In it I found the following words: "Remember to think of what you want, rather than what you fear." In many ways, that quotation characterizes what I have attempted to convey in this book: a way to think of what you want, a way to reduce the powers of your fears. For me, working with survivors has been a journey of discovery of the human spirit, of a person's capacity to love, and of myself. Collaborating with survivors has helped me to know myself and to grow. This book is my effort to return the favor. I hope that it helps you, the reader, to know yourself and to grow. You have my respect and my gratitude.

Sincerely,
Elizabeth G. Vermilyea

Introduction

Whom Is this Book For?

This workbook has been developed to help people learn specific skills for coping with the problematic after effects of past and present traumatic events. (A traumatic event is any situation that causes a person to experience stress so extreme that it overwhelms his or her natural ability to cope.) This workbook is intended for self-help users, but it is also extremely helpful for people who are currently in therapy. Think of it as a tool to help you deal with stress responses. It uses many ideas, techniques and skills developed in specialized work with people who have experienced severe trauma.

What Can this Book Do for You?

Over the years, I have taught self-regulation groups for **posttraumatic stress disorder (PTSD)** and **dissociation.** I have come to realize how many people have diffculties with emotions and painful experiences stemming from traumatic experiences. While most aspects of the book are geared toward people who have experienced traumatic stress as children, many of the exercises will be useful to people who are looking for a deeper self-understanding and who are exploring areas of life they may want to change. Everyone can use help where feelings are concerned, so another purpose of this workbook is to help readers understand their feelings and to provide concrete tools to help them manage these feelings and the effects of traumatic stress more effectively.

Posttraumatic stress disorder (PTSD)—a disorder that can develop when a person is exposed to traumatic events beyond their ability to cope; symptoms include intrusive experiences, avoidance experiences, and increased nervous system arousal (heightened nervous system activity).

Dissociation—a separation of the normally integrated or connected functions of identity, perception, personality, and memory.

How Do I Use the Workbook?

These materials can be used in three ways: as a self-help program, in one-on-one therapy, or in a group. You don't have to be in therapy to make use of the tools offered. However, it is important to follow each chapter in order the first time through. Each chapter builds on the one before it with regard to your understanding of the ideas, language, and exercises. To use this workbook most effectively, you will need:

- a separate notebook for journal writing
- art supplies
  - a blank book or notebook with no lines on the pages
  - crayons
  - modeling clay
  - colored pencils, markers, oil or chalk pastels.

Set aside time each day to work with this book. If you can, try to set aside the same time each day, or make some kind of schedule for yourself. Spend only as much time as you can comfortably stand. Start out spending only a few minutes daily, maybe working up to half an hour. Take each chapter slowly, working at your own pace. You don't have to complete a whole chapter in one sitting. In general, work on the skills in each chapter until they feel comfortable and familiar to you before moving on to the next chapter. It's okay if it takes you a few days or a few weeks. You may need to practice some skills for a few months before they become familiar. After you have been through the whole book, you may find it helpful to skip around and rework different chapters as you make progress with the skills.

The goal is to help you to understand some of the most common ways people deal with traumatic experiences, how these reactions to trauma feel, and how to cope with them. You don't have to understand traumatic stress for these tools to be helpful. You may find, however, that this book will teach you about how people respond to intense suffering and trauma.

A Note about Language

Every trade has its own "lingo," and mental health is no exception. The language used in this book is meant to be clear, effective, and inclusive. The terms used here come from the consumer/survivor self-help movement, the women's movement (for men using this workbook: don't be put off, because the women's movement offers a good model of empowerment), the medical community, and from various other points of view. The terms chosen are the most useful in describing the strategies taught in this workbook. For example, the terms *stress response*, *symptom*, and *adaptation* can all mean the troublesome effects of trauma and the coping skills people use to manage the trauma.

Some of the language in this book may be new to you. For this reason, we are including a glossary (which is like a little dictionary) at the back of the book. The glossary explains the meaning of the words that are special to mental health and trauma. It is important to understand and to learn to use some of these specialized terms. This way, you will know what is going on, and be able participate when treatment professionals talk their "lingo."

Is This Book for Me?

The following overview of the effects of traumatic experiences is meant to help you decide whether this book is for you. You may decide that it does *not* apply to you, or that it does, or that you are scared of what it may mean. If it does apply to you, I hope that this book can help you move forward in your recovery.

What Is Trauma?

In this workbook, the term *trauma* refers to severe neglect, emotional, physical and/or sexual abuse, as well as physical and sexual assault. Trauma may also encompass the effects of long-term separation from caregivers, repeated childhood hospitalization or medical procedures, or any other horrible experience that feels totally overwhelming. The term *traumatic stress* describes the effects of traumatic experiences. While *psychological trauma* is defined differently by various experts in the field, it is generally understood as a wounding to a person's sense of self and general well being. It is essential to understand that an individual's *own experience* determines whether an event is or is not traumatic.

Psychological trauma is the unique individual experience of an event or enduring conditions, in which

1. The individual's ability to make sense of his/her feelings is overwhelmed, or

2. The individual experiences a threat to life, body, or sanity. (Pearlman & Saakvitne, 1995, paraphrased)

A traumatic event or situation thus creates psychological trauma when it overwhelms the individual's perceived ability to cope, and leaves that person fearing that s/he will be hurt, killed, or go insane. The individual feels emotionally, mentally, and physically overwhelmed during the event. The circumstances of the event commonly include (1) abuse of power and betrayal of trust by the abuser, and (2) feelings of being trapped, helplessness, pain, confusion, and/or loss on the part of the victim. That is not to say that a trauma survivor feels this way all of the time, but that these are defining aspects of a traumatic experience. This definition of trauma is fairly broad, and it intentionally does not allow others to determine whether a particular event is traumatic; that evaluation is up to each survivor. In other words, *trauma is defined by the experience of the survivor.* Two people could undergo the same horrible event and one person might be traumatized while the other person remains relatively unharmed. Trauma comes in many forms, and people naturally cope in different ways. However, there are similarities and patterns of responses that cut across the variety of experiences and victims, so it is important to think broadly about trauma.

A person's natural ability to cope with a traumatic event is shaped by a number of factors, all of which help determine the lasting effects of a traumatic event:

1. whether the person survived a single traumatic incident vs. repeated trauma,

2. the age when the trauma occurred or began,

3. the source of the trauma—natural vs. human-made, and

4. the nature of the trauma—accidental vs. purposeful.

Single Blow vs. Repeated Trauma

In her studies of traumatized children, Lenore Terr has made the distinction between single blow and repeated traumas. Single shocking events can certainly produce trauma reactions in some people: among these events are natural disasters (such as earthquakes, hurricanes, and floods) technological disasters (such as auto and plane crashes, chemical spills, nuclear failures), and criminal violence (such as robbery, rape, and the witnessing of homicide).

As traumatic as single-blow traumas are, the traumatic experiences that result in the most serious mental health problems are repeated and extend over a long period of time, sometimes over years of a person's life. Ongoing child abuse, neglect, combat, urban violence, battering relationships, repeated losses, and enduring poverty are traumatic experiences that frequently result in prolonged mental health difficulties.

Age at the Time of Trauma

Posttraumatic stress condition—troubling or disruptive thoughts, feelings or impulses resulting from one or more traumatic experiences.

In our society, survivors of childhood abuse make up the largest number of people suffering from **posttraumatic stress conditions.** The scope of childhood trauma is staggering. Every day children are beaten, burned, slapped, whipped, thrown, shaken, kicked, and raped. According to Dr. Bruce Perry (1994), a conservative estimate of the numbers of children exposed to a traumatic event each year exceeds 4 million. The age at which trauma occurs or begins has an effect on recovery. However, even those who experience trauma at young ages can heal and recover.

Natural vs. Human-Made

Stressor—a particular event or experience that requires the use of coping skills; traumatic stressors are particular traumatic events or experiences that overwhelm adaptive coping skills.

Prolonged **stressors,** especially harm that is deliberately inflicted by people, are far harder to bear than accidents or natural disasters. Most people who seek mental health treatment for trauma have been victims of interpersonal violence (violence inflicted on them by another person). If the acts were done deliberately, in the context of an ongoing relationship, the problems are increased. The most diffcult situation is when the injuries are caused deliberately in a relationship with a person on whom the victim is dependent or trusts completely—most specifically a parent-child relationship.

Accidental vs. Purposeful

The effects of surviving a hurricane or a car accident are fundamentally different from the effects of surviving interpersonal violence. Accidental trauma, or "Acts of God," can be extremely terrifying, but intentional, interpersonal violence adds a new aspect to the experience. The sense that terror, pain, and suffering are no longer random is significant. Deliberate victimization or **sadistic** abuse has a powerful effect on the victim. When one person takes pleasure from hurting another vulnerable person, shame inevitably enters into the interaction. Shame enters into the equation with the victim experiencing deep feelings of humiliation at the hands of the victimizer. These feelings are usually increased if the abuser is someone who is supposed to care for the victim in some way. This may include a parent, relative, or clergy person.

Sadism (Sadistic)—pleasure derived from inflicting pain or cruelty on someone else.

The Effects of Bonding/Attachment

Early childhood trauma affects people deeply, especially trauma at the hands of caregivers. In the same way that good parenting is the ideal buffer against trauma, neglectful and/or abusive parenting causes the most devastating traumas. Children need strong, healthy **bonding** to caregivers in order to grow, flourish and mature. If early childhood relationships do not create safe, strong bonding, a child may experience lasting difficulty with forming and maintaining interpersonal relationships. Infants are born with the natural ability to form secure bonds. If bonding is disrupted, it is *never* the infant's/child's fault.

Bonding—developing a stable and supportive relationship with a primary caregiver; see *attachment*.

The Trauma Response

Clearly, more severe abuse is associated with more psychological disturbance. Severity may be based on (1) whether the violence is ongoing, (2) the degree of emotional closeness or trust in the victim's relationship with the abuser, (3) whether support or punishments result from telling someone about it; or (4) the victim's feelings of helplessness and fear of injury or death. Repeated early childhood trauma is especially damaging in the ways that it interrupts emotional and physical growth and development.

One of the best-documented research findings in the field of trauma is the *dose-response* relationship—the more traumas someone experiences, the more potentially damaging the effects. The greater the stressor, the more likely the development of PTSD. The effects of trauma are likely to be most severe if the trauma is repeated, experienced in childhood, man-made, unpredictable, multi-faceted, inflicted with deliberate intent, and perpetrated by a caregiver (Allen, 1995). Some people survive traumatic experiences unaffected at first, only to find that the experiences come back to haunt them months or years later. Some people have no memory of childhood trauma until they are adults. Some people who were traumatized in childhood have always remembered their traumatic experiences and have always felt trapped by the memories. All of these situations are natural responses to traumatic events. If trauma occurs early, and is caused by a trusted person with a desire to hurt, the chance of having ongoing problems is increased.

In focusing on psychological trauma, it is important to keep in mind that stress reactions affect the body as well. Traumatic events (especially those repeatedly experienced in childhood) affect your brain, mind, spirit, and body. During traumatic experiences, you do whatever you can to protect yourself. The **"fight or flight"** instincts may kick in, making you extra sensitive to danger. Adrenaline and other stress hormones flood your body, readying you to run for safety. Or perhaps you figure out (consciously or unconsciously) ways to avoid facing the danger: by getting drunk or by "zoning out." Either way, people work hard at self-protection, in whatever forms it may take.

Fight or Flight Response—a physiological response to perceived danger that activates the mind and body to defend or to flee.

Growing Beyond Survival

Crash Course in Child Development and Coping

Infancy

You have two sets of coping skills: those you are born with and those you learn. You are born with coping abilities that are both natural and highly functional. Your inborn coping abilities are designed to help you comfort and draw attention to yourself or to help you to reach out when self-comfort is not enough. During infancy, children are either content (comfortable) or distressed (upset). Distress is felt in the body and is not really a mental or cognitive experience. Infants communicate distress by crying, which in most cases is a very effective attention-getting device. Most infants are easily calmed through physical comforting, such as being held close to the body and rocked. Babies come into the world with behaviors that promote connections to others. Sucking, clinging, grasping, smiling, laughing, and even crying help encourage bonding with caregivers. The urge toward bonding with caregivers is the infant's most important inborn trait.

However, babies need help from caregivers to develop additional self-soothing and coping skills. Bonded caregivers will teach growing children how to soothe and distract themselves when they are feeling upset. Then, when the caregivers are not available, their children will be able to comfort themselves. Growing children learn new methods of coping by watching others and through active teaching from the caregivers. They learn to soothe themselves and to reach out when they are scared or confused. In healthy bonding, children learn to rely on themselves at times. At other times, especially when they are anxious, scared, or confused, babies will seek out and rely on parents in order to feel better. At first, nearly all of the soothing is provided by the caregivers and by soothing objects (e.g., blankets and stuffed animals). This allows children to internalize, or to mentally hold on to, the things that provide comfort. Over time, those connections will allow them to self-soothe independently, even in the absence of caregivers.

Toddlerhood

As children grow older and move into the toddler stage, distress is still largely felt in the body and is therefore usually expressed physically (i.e., through temper tantrums). Loving caregivers can help children identify feelings, talk about them, let them out and let feelings go. They can also help distract children from upsetting feelings so that they can focus on less distressing matters. Caregivers will also set limits on what kind of behavior is or isn't okay when children feel bad (for example, talking about feeling angry is okay but hitting people is not).

Pre-Adolescence (Elementary School Age)

Nurturance—promotion of development, teaching, training.

During pre-adolescence, a child's ability to cope and manage distress requires continued support and **nurturance.** The "fight or flight" response is active and functional. Feeling threatened leads to immediate emotional and bodily responses that start self-defense, safety, or escape behaviors. At this stage of life, children need ongoing, consistent help with managing their emotional responses. Their ability to manage frustration, sadness, anger, and fear is limited, and they can be easily overwhelmed, especially if they are hungry, tired, or in any way physically uncomfortable.

Adolescence (Teen Age)

Adolescence presents additional challenges for the young person who is trying to manage feelings. Changes in the body and social roles make emotions even more unstable and difficult for adolescents. Parents and caregivers walk a fine line at this stage, offering support and guidance while allowing adolescents to increase independence and to develop a separate sense of who they are. Helping young people recognize physical signs of stress becomes very important as teens may keep feelings hidden even from themselves. Providing a sense of safety and caring in which they can learn to name their feelings is extremely important. Safety, in this sense, refers to the knowledge that teens are accepted and won't be teased or put down.

This critically important work of helping children cope and grow into healthy adults needs to take place in a reliable, consistent, loving relationship. In a healthy environment, the caregivers are willing to live with most of the discomfort in the relationship and are not threatened by the relationship with the child. In an abusive or neglectful environment, caregivers may fail at many levels, starting with a failure to respond to the natural efforts of the child to attach. Neglectful or abusive caregivers may fail to attend to basic needs, or may leave the child to self-soothe all of the time. Caregivers may not respond to the child's efforts to reach out, and the child may give up. Caregivers may fail to teach the child additional coping skills, or may create confusing, inconsistent, chaotic, and even unspoken rules about when, where, and how any nurturing takes place. Finally, abusive or neglectful caregivers may model violence and/or self-harm as acceptable coping methods.

When children feel hurt, they need help to deal with their feelings. In the absence of help from caregivers, children are left with only the inborn coping mechanisms that may include rocking and trance-inducing behaviors. Children naturally and easily blur the boundaries between real and make-believe. In some traumatic home environments, it may be unsafe to express emotion. In those cases, children learn how not to feel or how to make feelings go away. In extreme circumstances, they may need to retreat completely into a make-believe world in order to escape, cope, and self-soothe. Children who are frequently left to manage as best they can will often turn to fantasy and avoidance. In extreme circumstances, they may cope through dissociation. Dissociation does occur naturally. Daydreaming is one example. However, dissociation used as a coping mechanism for traumatic experiences is a way of shutting something out so completely that is seems like it never happened. It can allow the child to move intolerable thoughts, feelings, and knowledge out of awareness. If shutting things out is the main way a person deals with pain, the reaction may become automatic and may happen outside of the child's control. These efforts to cope and protect one's sense of self are *natural* responses to a traumatic experience or environment.

Traumatic experiences have a powerful effect on emotions. Painful experiences (both physical and psychological) can lead to scary emotional states. In the absence of healthy emotional development, it becomes very difficult to identify, tolerate, or control the intensity of emotions. It may be very difficult to think and feel at the same time.

As neglected or abused children reach adolescence, they may turn to other methods of coping in order to self-soothe or escape pain. Pre-adolescent and adolescent girls are especially susceptible to harming their bodies (e.g., through cutting or burning) to relieve emotional pain. The development of eating disorders is an effort to exert control over *something*. Boys may become outwardly violent and disruptive, or may withdraw completely and become "loners." Pre-adolescent and adolescent trauma survivors are at *great risk* for substance abuse and addictions. Having little or no help with managing feelings, young people will use whatever means they can find to gain a moment's relief. The lasting impact of childhood trauma may be that the best attempts to cope during childhood begin to interfere with healthy connections and coping in adulthood.

Research is showing that traumatic memories are stored in the brain differently from non-traumatic memories. Traumatic memories are stored with high levels of emotion and seem to remain unchanged over time. They are frequently re-experienced as **flashbacks,** intrusive recollections of past

Flashback—an intrusive and vivid recollection of a traumatic experience, at times so realistic that it becomes difficult to tell whether the traumatic experience is happening in the moment or not, may involve one or more of the five senses (sight, taste, smell, touch, or hearing).

Crash Course in Child Development and Coping

traumatic events (repeated, unwanted, and unwelcome thoughts, images, or feelings related to the trauma). Extreme emotion has an interesting effect on memory. It may highlight a memory, making it extremely vivid, or it may inhibit recollection, making it very hard to remember. Trauma survivors frequently experience periods of too much memory contrasted by periods of too little memory. Additionally, if a person had dissociated during traumatic events, the memory may be distorted in other ways. Keep in mind that dissociation is an effort to adapt to and cope with overwhelming traumatic experiences. The stress of the trauma coupled with the effort to put it out of awareness is bound to affect a person's memory of the experience. In addition to memory disturbance, trauma can disrupt a person's sense of who he or she is; the ability to have satisfying, mutual relationships; the ability to recognize danger; the ability to take care of and nurture one's body; and the ability to control impulses.

Crash Course in the Frustrated Fight or Flight Response

In the absence of help, self-protective mechanisms can become problematic over time. Brain chemicals and the adaptive techniques that work with short periods of intense stress can backfire when traumatic stress is prolonged. When the fight-or-flight response is repeatedly activated but not acted upon, that response pattern is altered. That alteration will continue to affect the ability to cope with stress over time. Efforts to adapt are based on an attempt to bridge a gap between how things are and a person's *ability to handle* how things are. If that gap is too wide, people may use extraordinary measures to adapt.

In the process of adapting to extreme circumstances, survivors may develop methods of coping that are effective in the short run but harmful over a long period of time. In traditional mental health settings, these problematic adaptations are called symptoms. Survivors may prefer to think of them as adaptations, coping methods, escape routes, and so on, but regardless of what they are called, they can make life miserable especially when they cause difficulties with perceptions, feelings, and behaviors. When early efforts to cope with traumatic experiences result in present-day dysfunction, it is time to make some changes.

Healthy bonding in early childhood is the best buffer against the painful long-term effects of traumatic experiences, but many do not grow up in healthy families. Anyone with determination, hard work, and an experienced guide can develop the skills to overcome unhealthy traumatic stress responses. But survivors of early childhood trauma within the family have a greater challenge. They have to start at the beginning, rebuilding a stronger foundation than they possessed originally. Many survivors who have learned to use the tools in this book agree that the outcome has been worth the work. If you would like to read more about the long-term effects of childhood trauma, read Jon Allen's excellent book, *Coping with Trauma*, available at your library or from the Sidran Bookshelf catalog, which is available on the Sidran website or by request through the mail.

At this point you may wonder whether your experiences qualify as having been "traumatic" and whether you still suffer from the effects of those experiences. Certainly not everyone who experiences a trauma will develop difficulties or symptoms. Similarly, not all difficulties stem from traumatic experiences. It can be helpful to educate yourself about stress responses and traumatic stress conditions in order to understand more about your coping style and skills. The next few pages can help you to do just that.

Traumatic Stress Inventory

What Are Traumatic Stress Conditions?

Some (not all) people who are exposed to traumatic events develop coping styles that, though useful at the time of the trauma, become problematic in the long run. It can be hard to see that something that "works" can also be unhealthy. Take smoking, for example (at the risk of stepping into the great smoking debate). Smoking is a great example of something that "works" to help people relax, but almost everyone knows that it is an unhealthy habit. There are clear short-term "benefits" to smoking, but in the long run, it is harmful to the body. Unhealthy ways of coping with trauma are referred to by the mental health system as traumatic stress conditions or disorders. (Unhealthy coping through smoking can later lead to emphysema.) The most common of the traumatic stress conditions is Posttraumatic Stress Disorder. That means that the stress response symptoms become problematic after ("post") the trauma is over.

What Is Posttraumatic Stress Disorder (PTSD)?

Posttraumatic Stress Disorder is a condition that results after a person has experienced or witnessed an event or events that involved

- actual, threatened, or perceived death or serious injury, or
- a threat to the physical well being of him or herself or others; and
- a reaction of intense fear, helplessness, or horror. (DSM IV, p. 209)

Some of the stress responses people commonly experience after such a trauma are listed below.

Traumatic Stress Responses

Psychological Arousal (Overactive nervous system)

☐ Hypervigilance—constantly on the lookout for danger
☐ Exaggerated startle reflex—easily startled, cannot get used to sudden sounds
☐ Poor concentration—inability to focus or pay attention to tasks
☐ Sleep disturbances—inability to get to sleep or to stay asleep, or sleeping too much, or fear of going to sleep
☐ Irritability or outbursts of anger—having little tolerance for frustration, yelling with little provocation, expressing anger in inappropriate ways or at inappropriate times

☐ Panic attacks—sudden feelings of fear or terror accompanied by an increase in heart rate and pulse, rapid breathing, sweating, and thinking fearful thoughts

Intrusive Recollections

☐ Nightmares about the event
☐ Sudden onset of intense emotion
☐ Flashbacks—acting or feeling as if the trauma event is recurring; reliving the trauma as if it were happening now
☐ Preoccupation with the trauma, inability to be distracted from thinking about it
☐ Hallucinations—repeatedly seeing or hearing the parts of the trauma (may include images, sounds, smells, and thoughts)

Numbing/Avoidance Stress Responses

☐ Dissociation—a reduced awareness of one's self and/or the environment
☐ Depersonalization—feeling detached or separate from others or one's own body
☐ Disorientation—feeling dazed
☐ Amnesia—forgetting what has happened
☐ Confusion—inability to think clearly or to focus thoughts
☐ Isolation—withdrawal from people and activities that are typically a part of your life
☐ Denial—rejection of the idea that something is wrong
☐ Numbing—inability to feel your body or your emotions

Physical Stress Responses

☐ Nausea or other stomach problems
☐ Muscle tension, joint pain
☐ Fatigue
☐ Headaches
☐ Weakness
☐ Chronic fatigue, Fibromyalgia

Additional Responses

☐ Self-harming behaviors, self-mutilation
☐ Difficulties with sexuality, promiscuity, or denial of sexuality
☐ Substance use/abuse

Traumatic Stress Self-Test

1. Review the list just given, and put a check mark next to the stress responses you currently experience.

2. Are these stress responses better, worse or about the same as they have always been?

_____

3. Which of the stress responses give you the most trouble (happen most frequently)? Which are most distressing to you?

_____

_____

_____

4. How are these experiences currently interfering with your life (e.g., are you too scared to leave the house)?

_____

_____

_____

5. Are there times when these difficulties are more severe? When? Times when they are less severe? When?

_____

_____

_____

6. What do you typically do when these stress responses get worse?

_____

_____

_____

7. Are there any changes you would like to make in the ways you handle these experiences? If so, what are they?

_____

_____

_____

8. How do you imagine your life would be different if you could manage these experiences differently?

_____

_____

_____

_____

What Is Dissociation?

Dissociation is a normal process that everyone experiences to one degree or another. People daydream, or experience highway hypnosis ("zoning out" while driving). Children frequently become absorbed in stories or movies to the point that they don't notice what is going on around them. Children can become very involved in pretending and make-believe. All of these are normal types of dissociation. It is also normal to detach or dissociate under highly stressful or threatening conditions. This is seen when memory or perception of time is distorted in dangerous situations such as combat or assault. It makes sense that the mind is able to protect itself in situations where the body cannot escape. Some people who have experienced severe, repeated trauma (especially during childhood) may become very skilled at using dissociation as a coping technique to manage the overwhelming traumatic experience. During repeated abuse, dissociation solves a number of problems. By shutting out information about emotional and physical pain and even awareness of the event itself, dissociation allows a survivor to continue to function in the dangerous environment as if nothing is wrong. But if dissociation takes on a life of its own and interferes with a person's ability to get along on a day-to-day basis, it has become disruptive or a dissociative disorder.

Dissociative Disorder

Dissociation can become a problem if it begins to happen outside of a person's control. When a person can't come back from the daydream or cannot focus at all when driving, dissociation has taken over. This doesn't happen without a reason. Problematic dissociation almost always occurs in connection with some kind of repeated, overwhelming, traumatic experiences. Such experiences can range from abuse or combat to repeated medical procedures in early childhood.

It is common for people suffering with PTSD to dissociate without having the full range of symptoms associated with a dissociative disorder. Also, people may develop dissociative symptoms without PTSD. Some people have brief episodes of dissociation that aren't related to psychiatric disorders at all. However, children who dissociate to cope with traumatic events are likely to continue dissociating into adulthood and are more likely to develop a dissociative disorder that continues into adulthood. Single traumatic events rarely lead to a dissociative disorder. Some examples of dissociation due to trauma include

● Seeing the trauma happening to your body while you are watching from the ceiling,

- Focusing on a wallpaper pattern so intently that you are no longer there, or

- Disappearing into a bird that flies you out of the window and away from the trauma.

- Diving into a black hole where you feel nothing.

Dissociative Identity Disorder (DID)

DID is a type of dissociative disorder in which a person develops other identities inside to manage traumatic experiences. DID is developed in childhood and is identified with severe physical and sexual abuse as well as other repeated traumas (such as repeated painful medical procedures accompanied by extended separation from caregivers). Dissociation occurs along a continuum. That means that there are different degrees of dissociation. Degrees of dissociation range from mild (daydreaming) to intense (developing other identities inside). DID exists at the intense end of the continuum of dissociation and should be understood as a protective measure that is used when no other protective measures are available.

How Does a Dissociative Disorder Affect a Person?

For most people, the knowledge of who they are, the memories of what they have done in their lives, and how they see the world are somewhat connected or "associated." The ability to think about a memory and connect it to feelings and information about the memory is fairly continuous. Even if, at times, it is hard to recall some detail, the memory may "pop" up later. Dissociative disorders have the effect of reducing the ability to remember parts of traumatic events or feelings related to trauma in a protective manner. Dissociation is a skill that protects against unbearable pain and betrayal. The person may not remember things, or their memories may have a dream-like quality. Dissociation is a coping mechanism that saves lives. However, for many people, dissociation can become very problematic over time. Some of the ways people dissociate to survive traumatic experiences are listed below. If the list below seems to describe you, you may want to seek professional help. Dissociation is a difficult problem to manage by yourself.

Dissociative Adaptations

Memory Loss (Amnesia)

☐ Time loss—inability to recall significant periods of time during the day (e.g., getting up at 7:00 a.m. and then finding yourself at work at 11:00 a.m. without knowing what went on during the four hours.)

- [ ] Not remembering behavior—finding evidence of things you must have done, but you don't remember doing them
- [ ] Unexplained possessions—finding things you must have bought, but you don't remember buying them
- [ ] Fragmented memories of personal history—inability to remember significant parts of your past
- [ ] Fluctuation in skills—you can do some tasks easily sometimes, but at other times they are very difficult for you (e.g., sometimes you know how to play the piano, and sometimes you don't)

Hypnotic Stress Responses

- [ ] Spontaneous trance—the ability to focus your attention automatically to the point that you lose track of what's going on around you
- [ ] Enthrallment—being so caught up in some form of entertainment (e.g., a movie or book) that you feel as if you are a part of it
- [ ] Age regression—feeling like a little child, having the experience that everything else is bigger than you are, feeling much younger than your true age
- [ ] Negative hallucinations—the ability to make things "disappear" from your awareness (e.g., if someone is talking loudly, you may be able to concentrate to the point that you no longer hear the person saying anything; you may also be able to concentrate so that you can't see the person)
- [ ] Out-of-body experiences—having the experience of floating above your body, of not having a body or that your body is not a part of you, also feeling that you are not real

Process (Mental) Stress Responses

- [ ] Passive influence—feeling controlled from within, watching yourself do things you don't want to do
- [ ] Hallucinations—hearing voices in or outside of your head; seeing images in or outside of your head that are related to the voices or the trauma
- [ ] Referring to yourself as "we"—feeling like there are "others" inside your head
- [ ] Switching—moving into another personality or identity state; going away and letting "someone else" inside take over

Affective (Emotional) Stress Responses—stress responses related to mood and emotions

☐ Depressed mood—feeling hopeless and/or helpless, unable to enjoy things you used to enjoy and not knowing why

☐ Rapid mood swings—frequent and sudden changes in mood or emotion that aren't related to a present experience or event

Somatic (Physical) Stress Responses—stress responses related to your body

☐ Pseudo or psychogenic seizures—seizures that cannot be medically explained but seem to be related to the traumatic experiences; they may be an unconscious defense against or response to trauma

☐ Pain—experiencing real pain that has no medical origin

☐ Conversion—the process of feeling physical pain or discomfort instead of emotional pain and discomfort (e.g., when you get angry, the anger goes away immediately, but you have a migraine instead)

Dissociation Self-Test

1. Review the list just given, and put a check mark by the items you currently experience.

2. Are these episodes better, worse, or about the same as they have always been?

_____

3. Which of the items give you the most trouble? Which are most distressing to you?

_____

_____

_____

4. How are these experiences currently interfering with your life (e.g., perhaps you are too scared to leave the house)?

_____

_____

_____

5. Are there times when these difficulties seem more severe? When? Times when they are less severe? When?

_____

_____

_____

6. What do you typically do when these stress responses get worse?

_____

_____

_____

7. Are there any changes you would like to make in the ways you handle these experiences? If so, what are they?

_____

_____

_____

8. How do you imagine that your life would be different if you could manage these stress responses differently?

_____

_____

_____

Are Other Difficulties Associated with Trauma?

Other difficulties: Frequently people who have experienced traumatic stress in childhood report other problems related to their stress response. These include

- [ ] Eating problems
- [ ] Substance abuse
- [ ] Depression
- [ ] Anxiety/panic
- [ ] Problems in relationships
- [ ] Physical problems that doctors can't diagnose
- [ ] Self-harmful behavior, self-mutilation
- [ ] Sexual difficulties: promiscuity, dangerous sexual practices, or denial of sexuality

It is important to understand that these difficulties provide a way for you to understanding how you are handling traumatic experiences. They do not mean that you aren't trying hard enough or that you are manipulative. Eating problems and substance abuse often are methods that people use when they try to reduce their internal distress or pain. Depression, anxiety/panic and problems with relationships are frequently the results of trauma and should not be seen as flaws in a person's character. If someone has a fever from an infection, would you consider it to be a character flaw? Probably not. The struggles people have from early childhood traumas need to be regarded in the same way. As with a fever, there are things people can do to reduce the severity of stress responses and recover from them. However, as with a fever, people have to take responsibility for taking good care of themselves in order to recover.

What Can I Do about All of These Experiences?

Many people have asked this question and have found a way to a life in recovery and healing. While traumatic experiences are painful and can cause people a great deal of difficulty, there are some well-documented methods for addressing trauma responses and improving daily life. Start with the basics.

Basic tools

Basic tools can be used immediately! Even though managing the effects of traumatic stress will require some education and a lot of hard work, there are things you can do *now* to help yourself. Each skill will be described in detail throughout the chapters of this book. These skills are the foundations of traumatic stress management and are crucial tools in recovery.

Grounding—Present, here-and-now awareness. Grounding is the process of connecting with the present moment so that you can connect with your resources and options. Grounding involves two distinct factors: awareness *and* connectedness.

Reality check—The process of accurately figuring out what is really happening in the moment versus what you may *think* or *feel* is happening. A reality check requires making a *huge* effort to seek out help from inside and outside sources and to accept the help that is available to you.

Feelings check—Paying attention to and learning the natural cycle of increases and decreases in feelings and mood states.

Imagery—Using your imagination to manage difficult experiences. Imagery allows you to plan or problem solve, to achieve a goal, and to comfort yourself.

Journal writing—Writing to facilitate self-awareness, understanding, self-expression, healing and recovery.

Artwork—Drawing to facilitate self-awareness, understanding, self-expression, healing, and recovery.

Talking—Using words to describe your thoughts, feelings, and experiences to yourself and to others. *Self-talk* is a very important part of recovery.

Now that we have defined some of the terms used throughout this workbook, it is necessary to review the goal of this handbook. *The purpose of this book is to help you increase self-awareness and understanding as well as promote healing and recovery from traumatic stress responses.* In order to do that, you'll need to address three basic questions about the effects of your traumatic experiences and the adaptations you have developed to manage them.

The Three Questions Are

1. What are your current traumatic stress responses (symptoms)? Where do they come from, and why are they happening now?

2. What do your stress responses feel like? What is your experience of them?

3. How can you learn to recognize and manage these stress responses, as well as to decrease their frequency and intensity?

Each chapter will address the development of traumatic stress adaptations, the ways in which those adaptations are experienced, and management techniques to ultimately reduce the effects of trauma sufficiently for you to live life the way you want to.

Stress Responses

The introduction to this workbook may have seemed overwhelming. You may be asking yourself whether you can still get a refund on this book! But, take this moment to become aware of any stress you are feeling right now. Use the worksheet to help yourself focus and put aside some of this stress.

1. Are there any obstacles you can think of that would keep you from working on your stress responses right now?

_____
_____
_____
_____

2. Can you take a moment to put those obstacles, fears, or concerns on the back burner so that you will be able to approach this material with fewer worries?

Example

```
I leave my fears about change
in this box for now.
```

Take whatever you can put aside and write about or draw it in the box below. It will be waiting there whenever you want it

The Toolbox

Tools of the Trade

Working on machinery requires proper tools. Working on yourself requires nothing less. Some of the physical tools are:

- journal book
- art book, pens/pencils
- clay
- markers.

Some of the mental tools are

- willingness
- concentration
- pacing
- and self-acceptance.

Managing traumatic stress and growing beyond survival are tasks that will take you on a journey of conflict and acceptance into places of pain and hidden strength. This journey can change your life.

What to Expect

Expect to feel worse before you feel better. Becoming more self-aware means coming into contact with feelings you have been avoiding or that you had to shut away to protect yourself. The only reason you avoided those feelings is because they hurt! You will need to experience those feelings in order to heal them. At times, this will not feel good, but it is necessary. The key (and the focus of this section) is to use these tools to help you manage the intensity of your feelings and the stress responses/adaptations they may trigger.

Expect to encounter internal **resistance**/roadblocks to change. This is 100% natural. Most people resist change, even when it is for the good. Change is scary. You will need to be patient and gentle with yourself and be aware of your own resistance. Understanding the fear will help you to overcome it. Understanding will need to come first. Bulldozing through fear isn't helpful when dealing with traumatic stress.

Expect some of these tools to begin working for you right away. They will help you feel more in control, less helpless, and therefore stronger inside. The more you practice with the tools, the more effective they will be. You will probably need to tailor the tools to suit your needs. Not all tools work for all people. Keep practicing until you find the best ones for you.

Resistance—in therapeutic terms, a natural tendency or instinctive opposition to change or exposure of things you store in your unconscious mind.

Self-regulation—the process of consciously managing different internal states by 1) experiencing them as they come up, 2) expressing what you are experiencing, 3) consciously postponing dealing with traumatic material or overwhelming aspects of feelings, and 4) retrieving part of what you have contained when you are better able to manage it.

In Jon Allen's words (1995), "Control is the antidote/cure for helplessness." Asking for help from trusted others is part of gaining control. This section of the workbook will introduce you to the tools that will help you learn to recognize when you need help, where to go for help, and how to gain control over the effects of your stress responses. The type of control that people find most helpful is known as **self-regulation.** Self-regulation will help you to increase self-awareness, access to options, and freedom to choose. Self-regulation sounds good but can be very difficult for people who have been coping primarily through avoidance. Anyone who has had to reduce self-awareness in order to cope with traumatic experiences will probably struggle (fight, kick and/or scream!) with the idea of *increasing* self-awareness: it will seem like the *wrong* thing to do. The tools in this section work. They have helped countless trauma survivors. They require determination and practice. Don't give up. Even if a technique only helps after the 50th time you try it, it still works!

The Idea of Self-Regulation

Self-regulation is a term that can cover the whole process of becoming more aware of emotions and other internal experiences. What you did with your obstacles in the beginning of the book was a form of self-regulation. *Self-regulation is about managing the intensity of feelings so that they don't take over.* If you completed Self-Regulation Worksheet 1 you increased your self-awareness, which is a lead-in to self-regulation. If the term *self-regulation* seems a bit stuffy, you can also think of it as self-management, or self-control. In any case, self-regulation also means being able to manage what you discover, as you become more aware. If you struggle to know what you are feeling most of the time, or have trouble managing strong feelings, your self-regulation skills can help you feel more in control of emotions without your having to shut them out completely. Having greater control of your emotions will also allow you to be more aware of pleasant feelings. After all, if you shut out uncomfortable feelings, the pleasant feelings can get shut out too.

Self-regulation begins with *noticing.* You can't regulate what you don't notice. Although your mind is the center of your awareness, your mind is complex and sometimes you may not notice things that are important. Your mind may wander. Maybe there are times when you cannot get something off your mind. You might not be able to stop thinking about something that worries you. You may *try* to focus your attention on a problem, but you can't seem to stay focused. You may have trouble remembering simple things. To begin practicing self-regulation, you need to understand some of the ways in which your mind works.

The diagram on this page can be used as a model of your mind. It may help you to get an idea of what happens when traumatic experiences are kept out of your awareness for long periods of time. Keep in mind that this diagram is only a *model.* It represents experiences rather than the actual mental processes at work.

In the next model, illustrated on page 26, the **conscious** mind represents present awareness of yourself and what is going on around you. The conscious mind is in touch with what is happening now. For example, you may be consciously aware of the temperature of the room you are in or of the noises outside. The **pre-conscious** represents things that can be remembered fairly easily or at least with a little effort, like phone numbers and addresses. The **unconscious** represents a place where information or awareness about yourself and your experiences is stored. This information is not

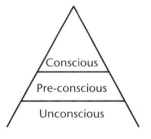

Model of the Mind

Conscious—present awareness

Pre-conscious—accessible memory.

Unconscious—inaccessible memory.

necessarily available to you in the usual way. *You can't necessarily get to it by trying to remember it.* Those embarrassing slips of the tongue are often said to have come from the unconscious.

Memories, feelings you can't stand, and motivations may exist in the unconscious where you don't notice them. Yet these parts of you still affect and sometimes control your behavior. When a person dissociates, some aspect of his or her experience may be stored away in the unconscious. The result is a feeling of time loss or amnesia. It's as if information has been stored in a memory bank but cannot be retrieved in the usual way. However, these memories that you can't get to may sometimes come up with no warning. As a result, there is often a problem with having no memory or feeling ("numbing") or having too much memory or feeling ("flooding").

Why Do I Shut Things Out?

Sometimes people who experience trauma will shut thoughts and feelings away in an effort to manage their intensely painful experiences. This kind of coping through reduced awareness is sometimes called *dissociation, numbing* or *avoidance.* Dissociation, numbing, and avoidance (shutting things out) is not necessarily done on purpose, and a person may not even realize that the process is happening. When people dissociate or numb out during trauma, their experience is stored in the brain in a different way from non-traumatic experiences. Information about thoughts, emotions, behavior, or physical feelings is disconnected and stored in the brain in such a way that a person may not be able to remember it very easily. This information can be lost or may be unavailable for a short or a long time. Some people find that information from years of their lives is unavailable to them. They simply can't remember. They may not even know that they have forgotten. Other people find that they do all kinds of things to keep memories of their trauma from coming up. In other words, they remember the trauma, but they try to numb out and avoid thinking about it. What they don't realize is that not dealing with the trauma (once they are safe) increases the power that the trauma has over them.

Coping through dissociation is usually quite rare. However, for people who have had traumatic experiences as children and have had little or no help coping with those experiences, dissociation, numbing, and avoidance may be the only ways to deal with the traumas and still remain sane. One of the problems with this method of coping is that the unconscious can, in a sense, "fill up"(not literally). Often as adults, people who have used dissociation, numbing and avoidance as their main coping mechanisms find that at some point, the methods stop working, and thoughts and feelings that relate to the trauma start to spill out or crop up. This can lead to a general increase in traumatic stress responses such as **anxiety, hypervigilance,** and visual images about the trauma.

For example, if you feel threatened and react to the threat in the same way that you did as a child, chances are that your reaction will reinforce the feeling of threat.

J. struggles with memories of abuse as a child. She often has the feeling that she is in danger, especially at night. No matter what she does, she can't make herself feel safe. Usually, when she feels scared or threatened, J. hides in her closet with the light off. She puts a blanket over her head and huddles as far into the corner as possible, just like when she was little and mommy was mad at her. Sometimes she falls asleep there and wakes up extremely disoriented and frightened. J. has trouble understanding why the closet feels safe sometimes and scary at other times. While in the closet, J. usually disappears into her mind or worries about whether or not someone will find her and hurt her.

In this example, J. is doing things that actually increase her fear. The fact that she hid in closets as a child is significant. But hiding as an adult makes the feelings of terror she had as a child stronger. At the same time that it makes her feel more threatened, exposed, and confused, the hiding also seems like a safe thing to do because it makes her focus on the terror of being found and hurt. The adaptation (hiding) is a reaction to the traumatic stress response (feeling threatened) that can actually *increase* the traumatic stress response (feeling exposed, helpless, and confused).

J's initial urges to hide end up creating more distress for her. Her hiding is an effort to shut down her awareness. While that may have been the only way for her to manage as a child, it may not be the best way to manage as an adult. Shutting down awareness as an adult increases risk of danger in many ways. In the outside world, hiding or reducing external awareness could put J. at greater risk of real outside threats as well as inside fearful thoughts and feelings. When survivors attempt to shut away awareness, this action often causes something else to come up or erupt. These "eruptions" are often experienced or understood as flashbacks or nightmares, and they can cause an increase in other disruptive experiences and posttraumatic responses.

A certain amount of dissociation is normal, but the kind that relates to traumatic events creates a block between you and information about things that threaten or frighten you. This type of dissociation can interfere with daily life. Over time, the method can stop working. When it begins to break down, you may find yourself experiencing thoughts and feelings related to the trauma, nightmares, or other scary experiences. Once this occurs, or

Anxiety—fearful feelings and negative thoughts about the future.

Hypervigilance—being on guard.

The Idea of Self-Regulation

when you feel a need to improve your quality of life, it is time to learn new ways of coping. Dissociation is no longer going to work the way it did.

Why Doesn't Shutting Things Out Work the Way It Used To?

The model below shows what can happen if you start to avoid feelings most of the time. Even new experiences become shut away. Eruptions increase. These eruptions bring into present awareness the very things you may be dissociating to avoid. The result is a vicious cycle. You end up dissociating to avoid the eruptions that dissociation causes! This cycle of traumatic stress responses can keep you from doing many things that you want or need to do.

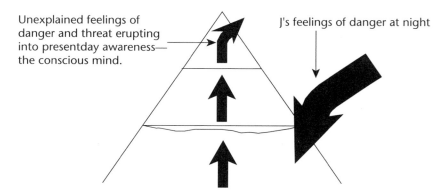

Unexplained feelings of danger and threat erupting into presentday awareness— the conscious mind.

J's feelings of danger at night

Old feelings of danger, memories of being hurt when mommy was mad.

Self-Regulation Worksheet 1

Exercises: Understanding the different parts of your mind.

1. Name three things that you are aware of right now (e.g., your conscious mind is aware of the warmth of the room).

_____   _____   _____

2. How do you know you are aware of these things? What evidence do you have? (e.g., your five senses provide information through vision, hearing, smell, etc.)

_____

_____

_____

3. Name three **non**-traumatic things that aren't usually in your awareness but that you can remember easily (e.g., your pre-conscious mind recalls your phone number or address).

_____   _____   _____

4. How do you go about becoming aware of those things? How do you bring them into your mind? (e.g., do you create images, or _think_ about them?)

_____

_____

_____

5. What kinds of things that are usually not in your mind that come into your mind outside of your control? (e.g., you suddenly might remember the loss of a loved one or pet.)

_____

_____

_____

6. What words do you use to describe where these things seem to come from?

_____

_____

_____

7. Which of the items below makes life harder for you,

    ❑ things you are presently aware of;
    ❑ things you can recall; or
    ❑ things that come into your mind outside of your control?

8. Are there any changes you would like to make about the way in which your mind is working these days? If so, what are they? If not, why not?

_____

_____

_____

The Idea of Self-Regulation

Cycle of Traumatic Stress Responses

The "Cycle of Traumatic Stress Responses" shows how avoidance, dissociative coping, and posttraumatic experiences can cause each other to create a sometimes constant feeling of being trapped in stress responses. A stress response can trigger avoidance in the form of denial, dissociation, bingeing, substance abuse, self-harm, and other behaviors in an effort to get rid of feelings. These avoidance behaviors, in turn, can trigger stress responses inside because they are reminders of old efforts to deal with painful feelings. The stronger the response, the stronger the impulses to avoid. The effort spent avoiding leaves little energy to manage day-to-day life, and the result is increased stress responses that increase the impulses to avoid. What a mess!

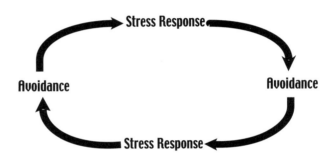

Fortunately, self-regulation skills can help you to tolerate (sit with) and control intense feeling states that have led to avoidance or dissociation in the past. You can learn to feel *and* control the intensity of your emotions to reduce avoidance. This will help reduce the frequency and intensity of traumatic stress symptoms and experiences. This handbook will teach you the relationship between dissociation, numbing, avoidance, and traumatic stress, and will help you to replace old, currently problematic coping (e.g., dissociation, avoidance, etc.) with conscious, more effective methods of coping (e.g. imagery, artwork, self-talk etc.).

The self-regulation recipe you will learn involves the following steps:

1. **Experience**—notice how you feel; notice pleasurable feelings as well as uncomfortable feelings, observe without judging; don't numb out and try not to make uncomfortable feelings worse; take note of what's going on inside.

Experience—the process of personally observing, encountering, or undergoing something.

2. **Express**—say something; tell yourself what you are noticing; write; draw your feelings; tell someone else who can listen supportively.

3. **Contain**—consciously postpone dealing with the overwhelming part of what you are experiencing; hold only what you can stand for a length of time and then put it aside; you will be storing these things in your pre-conscious instead of your unconscious.

4. **Retrieve**—later, when you are able (with a friend, in therapy, or with a journal), bring back a small part of what was stored and repeat the process of experiencing and expressing with that small piece.

These steps will be discussed at length throughout this book. None of the steps is easy, but each is important. The next chapter begins the work of identifying activities and telling how they work. Any questions that may have come up while reading through the initial pages will, I hope, be answered as you progress through each section. Aspects of the self-regulation recipe will be addressed in each chapter, so watch for those connections. Each skill chapter is broken up into the following sections: goals, ideas, skills, and activities. There will be plenty of space for working in this book and helpful hints along the way. Pace yourself!

Tool: Grounding

Goals: to increase awareness in the here and now; to facilitate clear reality contact; to reduce posttraumatic experiences (i.e., flashbacks, hypervigilance, and intrusive recollections) and to reduce dissociative experiences (i.e., spontaneous trance, depersonalization, time loss, and uncontrolled switching).

Ideas:

1. **Present focused awareness** is important for combating the avoidance that occurs through dissociation (spontaneous trance, uncontrolled switching, time loss, and depersonalization) and traumatic stress adaptations (numbing, avoidance, flashbacks, nightmares, and panic). If you are paying attention to the here and now, then you are less likely to be lost in the past with no awareness of present-day resources. In addition, you are also less likely to be caught up in fearful thoughts about the future. In the past, dissociation may have been the only defense against trauma; leaving the body was a helpful skill back then. It was too painful and/or dangerous for you to focus on experiences as they happened. In the present, however, shutting thoughts and feelings out or leaving your body re-creates the old fears and might make you feel just like you did as a child. Present focused awareness is your defense against becoming trapped in the hopeless and helpless feelings of the past.

2. **Grounding** is the process of being present and connected in the here and now. Stress responses can numb people so they don't experience the terror and the horror of trauma in the moment. Dissociation and numbing continue to reduce present awareness in an attempt to protect against overwhelming traumatic events and experiences. However, over time, the process of dissociation and numbing may fail or may interfere with everyday life. Survivors become aware of stress responses such as flashbacks. Dissociation and numbing were *wartime* survival techniques, and using wartime strategies during peacetime is not effective. Dissociation may have helped you to manage the unmanageable, but as an adult in peacetime, you need life skills rather than survival skills. Just like war veterans with PTSD who struggle to cope with peacetime living, you need to learn how to manage intense, overwhelming experiences in more present-focused ways.

B. had a traumatic childhood. He witnessed terrible fights between his parents and had to protect his brothers and sisters from his father. He was always afraid when he heard people yelling because to him it meant danger in

*his house. He used to "fade away" (trance out) whenever the yelling would
start so that he wouldn't have to be scared. Now, as an adult, B. can't go anywhere that might expose him to yelling because he becomes terrified and
"fades away" (trances out) almost automatically. B.'s inability to manage his
reactions to yelling severely restricts his life because he can't be around his
children when they yell, and he can't enjoy things like ball games because of
the yelling. Sometimes he hears yelling in his head, and he can't stop himself
from fading away. B.'s posttraumatic experiences (flashbacks) and wartime
coping mechanisms (fading away) are interfering with his peacetime life.*

B. can do several things to help himself. The first thing is to begin using
grounding tools with self-talk. B. will need to practice the tools almost constantly in order to combat the automatic numbing and dissociation that
takes over when he is "triggered" by the yelling.

Grounding Worksheet 1

Using Your Five Senses

- **Sight**—open your eyes; look around; name present-day sights; connect with them ("this is my driver's license," etc.); realize that you're an adult; look at how tall you are
- **Sound**—listen for present-day sounds and name them; let them bring you closer to the present; talk to yourself inside; say comforting things
- **Taste**—suck on a peppermint; chew gum; drink coffee; use tastes that are connected with being safe and being an adult; carry these things with you at all times
- **Smell**—use scented hand lotion, potpourri, a cotton ball soaked with perfume, or scented candles to remind you of the present, carry something with you that you can use anywhere
- **Touch**—hold a safe object; feel textures and let them bring you closer to the present; pet your cat or dog (or parrot!); connect with a loving presence in your life and let it help you remain in the present; carry a note or small object from someone you love

Items to Use for Grounding Yourself:

Sight	Sound	Smell	Taste	Touch
watch or clock	soothing music	scented candle	peppermint	lotion
photograph	nature sounds	potpourri	cinnamon	a stone
outdoors	familiar sounds	scented lotion	lemon	ice cube
driver's license	your voice	essential oils	chewing gum	pets

List some of the things you can do to get grounded using your five senses.

Sight (Example)—*When B. hears his children yelling, he can look at them and tell himself, "These are my kids, and it's natural for kids to yell; they are safe."*

_____

_____

Sound—*B. can learn to listen to the noise to identify what kind of yelling he's hearing. He can tell himself, "Those people are cheering. They are happy and excited. They aren't in danger."*

_____

_____

Taste—*B. likes the taste of cinnamon gum. He carries it with himself all of the time and can focus on the taste of the gum to help him feel more grounded.*

_____

_____

Smell—*B.'s wife uses Snuggle fabric softener in the laundry. When he plays with his kids, the smell of their clothes helps keep him focused on the present.*

_____

_____

Touch—*B. keeps a smooth piece of hematite rock in his pocket. He holds it when he feels scared.*

_____

_____

Tool: Grounding

What Are the Stress Responses that Interfere with Grounding? Why Do They Happen?

- Spontaneous trance (zoning out), switching, age regression (thinking you are getting little), flashbacks, hypervigilance (being on guard), numbing, and avoidance interfere with grounding by reducing self awareness and awareness of the present environment. People with traumatic stress responses or dissociation usually experience these processes when they feel frightened or threatened in some way. The reactions may happen so often that they feel like a normal part of life.

Why Should I Consider Other Kinds of Coping?

- Using dissociation to cope with present stressors frequently brings up the same feelings and perceptions you had in the past, making it hard to know that things are different today

- The traumatic connections that come up when you use old coping mechanisms (dissociation or numbing) also interfere with problem solving in the present.

- Your posttraumatic reactions can make you *feel* threatened even when you aren't actually threatened. The old ways of coping (dissociation or numbing) might make the feeling of threat stronger.

- If you remain focused in the past or fearful about the future, you may not be able to tell the difference between what you feel and what is really happening. You won't be able to remember that things are different now that you have helpers and resources. Remember that shutting things out today can increase the traumatic stress responses you will have later. Work to stay in the moment, right here, right now.

- Dissociation can keep a person emotionally trapped in the past. Dissociation interferes with emotional growth. This, in turn, makes it very difficult to have healthy relationships.

- Dissociation becomes problematic, and new coping skills need to be developed.

How Will I Know When I'm Having Traumatic Stress Responses?

- Learning about your stress responses will help you recognize them. Pay attention to yourself.

- Spontaneous trance may feel like you are fading or going away; like you are disappearing, disconnecting, or zoning out. You may also feel like you aren't real, or the world isn't real, or that you are drugged.

- Switching may feel like something or someone else is taking over, like you are slipping away, like you are moving out of the "hot spot," or like someone else inside is in control now. It may seem that there is a gap in what just happened or that you are filling in the blanks, picking up in the middle of things.

● Age regression may make you feel as if you are getting little or younger; everything else is getting big; your clothes don't fit; your hands appear too big; you feel helpless or very young and unable to talk. People may ask you, "What just happened?"

● Flashbacks may make you feel like you are experiencing some part of the trauma again. Initially it is common to experience flashbacks as intense emotions or physical pains that do not seem connected to anything in the present or past. You may be seeing (in your mind or in the environment) or hearing things related to trauma even though those things are not currently present in the environment (e.g., you hear the voice of your abuser even though he or she has been dead for years). You may be feeling physical pains that have no medical source, or smell things no one else smells.

● Hypervigilance feels like being on guard, needing to keep track of everything going on around you, jumping at every sound, or watching for the threat that you feel is there. This adaptation can make you feel threatened even when you are safe.

● Numbing may make you feel like you are separated from your body, or as if you have no body or no feelings.

● Avoidance may make you feel like you have to get away or ignore something. You may feel like you just can't deal with or discuss something; it's the wrong thing to do.

skills

What Should You Do When You Are Having a Traumatic Stress Response or a Dissociative Experience?

Mindfulness—paying attention to oneself, noticing what is going on inside.

● Grounding techniques are the methods used to increase **mindfulness.** They help you keep track of what is really going on inside yourself and in the environment. The basic tools will help you to know the following:

● **Who** you are—you are an adult in an adult body
● **Where** you are—location in the present
● **When** you are—the present day and date

● If you can answer these questions and connect with the answers, you are less likely to lose track of the differences between the past and the present. This is important because you will be less likely to have a flashback and will have fewer dissociative experiences.

 *Tool: Grounding*

● It is important to be able to focus on present reality no matter how you are feeling or what part of yourself is in control. In this way, you will be grounded when you are happy, sad, angry, feeling little, or in a different identity state. This will help you to control disruptive experiences and have a more satisfying life. Without grounding, you can feel like a real free-for-all inside, and sometimes outside too.

Grounding Worksheet 2

Identify some situations, feelings, and thoughts that let you know you aren't very grounded (e.g., staring while driving, feeling disconnected, thinking that you're not real).

_____

_____

_____

Now, identify *things* that help you feel grounded or *times* you know you are grounded (e.g., my pet helps me focus on the present; or I'm usually grounded at school).

_____

_____

_____

If you're trying to get more grounded and more focused on the present, some things help and some things that make it harder. Look at the lists below for ideas about dos and don'ts.

✗ Don't:

Trance: Remember to identify and avoid any repetitive behaviors like rocking, staring, humming or anything else you have done in the past to "check out, go away," or dissociate.

Think scary thoughts: focusing on things that will increase fear, helplessness, hopelessness or anxiety will increase the urge to dissociate.

✔ Do:

Look around
Breathe deeply
Move your arms and legs
Say comforting things to yourself
Think about people, places or
things that you are positively connected to

List some reasons why you think you shouldn't be grounded (e.g., feelings are too threatening).

_____

_____

_____

Are they reasons that you had in the past? Do you think some of them may no longer apply in the present? If so, which ones rarely occur or no longer apply?

_____

_____

_____

List reasons you want or need to be grounded (e.g., to improve functioning).

_____

_____

_____

_____

 *Tool: Grounding*

Grounding Worksheet 3

It is much easier to make intrusive experiences go away if you are grounded. Intrusive experiences are things that we hear, see, and sense in other ways that aren't really happening in the present but that probably come from our memory of the past (for example, seeing someone who isn't there but who seems real, feeling intense emotions for no apparent reason).

What can you say to yourself when this is happening? What can you say to feel more grounded and less scared? The following may give you some ideas. Add some of your own suggestions.

This is a symptom, a traumatic stress response
This feels real but is coming from my head
Who inside is causing this? What do you need?
What is this experience telling me?
Is there something I might enjoy doing?

_____

_____

_____

Write down what you hear and what you think people mean when they encourage you to get more grounded. Then practice checking it out by asking what they mean.

_____

_____

_____

Are these messages similar to messages from the past? _____ Yes _____ No
Do you think that the messages are coming from others today or from your head? How can you tell the difference (e.g., do a reality check)?

_____

_____

_____

Identify three goals related to grounding that you can concentrate on practicing daily.

1._____

2._____

3._____

Tool: Grounding

Grounding Worksheet 4

Use this sheet to keep track of how focused or grounded you are for a whole week. Put a number from 1 to 10 in each box, for each hour. Indicate how grounded you are. The numbers 1, 2, or 3 would show that you aren't very grounded; 4, 5, or 6 would show that you are moderately grounded; and 7, 8, 9, or 10 would indicate that you are mostly grounded.

Not grounded 1————————5————————10 Very grounded

	Sunday	Monday	Tuesday	Wednesday	Thursday	Friday	Saturday
8:00 a.m.							
9:00 a.m.							
10:00 a.m.							
11:00 a.m.							
12:00 p.m.							
1:00 p.m.							
2:00 p.m.							
3:00 p.m.							
4:00 p.m.							
5:00 p.m.							
6:00 p.m.							
7:00 p.m.							
8:00 p.m.							
9:00 p.m.							
10:00 p.m.							

Do you notice any patterns (days of the week, times of day) to your dissociative adaptations? If so, what are they?

_____

_____

Are these patterns meaningful to you? Do they relate to past experiences? How so?

_____

_____

Do the patterns relate to present-day stressors? How so?

_____

_____

_____

_____

_____

 Tool: Grounding

Tool: Reality Checks

Reality Checks are tools to help you become aware of and connected to the facts about what is really happening. They should be used when you experience old familiar feelings that remind you of the ways you used to feel when you were in a dangerous situation or environment. Reality checks involve paying attention to your own reactions in relation to events around you. They also involve being able to assess safety accurately and involve resources to help you determine whether you are in danger and, if so, how you will get help or reduce your risk.

- **What** has just happened?
- **Who** was involved in terms of present-day people?
- **Which** stress responses are you experiencing right now?
- **Where** are your resources?
  - Internal resources: self-talk, strengths, ability to express feelings
  - External resources: friends, therapist, hotline, 911
- **How** can you get help right now if you need it?

Use the following worksheets to become familiar with different ways of doing reality checks.

 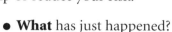

Reality Check Worksheet

When you are struggling to connect with reality, use the following format to help ground yourself. These questions may be used before, during, or after working on grounding techniques.

1. **What** has just happened? (Just the facts, don't judge the situation.)

_____
_____
_____

2. **Who** was involved in terms of present-day people?

_____
_____
_____

3. **Whom** did they remind you of? Did you confuse them with someone from the past? If so, who?

_____
_____
_____

4. **Which** stress responses are you experiencing right now? (Use the inventories from pp. 8–9 & 12–14)

_____
_____
_____

5. **Where** are your resources right now?
_Internal_____
_____
_____

_External_____
_____
_____

How can you get help right now if you need it? What do you need to do? Whom do you need to call? Keep a list handy so it's there when you need it.

_____
_____
_____
_____
_____

"It's okay not to know all of the answers right now. This takes practice. Sometimes just asking the question can be an important step. Begin to trust in yourself. You can become your own strongest and most consistent resource in time."—S.M. (Consumer/Survivor/Advocate)

 Tool: Reality Check

40

What If I'm Scared, and I Don't Want to Be Grounded and More Aware?

Dissociation can be confusing today as an adult. It may create a sense of safety or protection without actually providing safety. In fact, dissociation can make people more vulnerable to danger because it frequently blocks the ability to connect with internal and external resources in the present. These resources are new, perhaps, and may not have been available before. Dissociation often takes people closer to the unconscious mind, closer to the very things they may be dissociating to avoid. This can result in a general increase in traumatic experiences. Survivors can expect grounding to *feel* wrong at first, but it is still an essential part of recovery. With practice, grounding will help you to feel safer.

No one doubts the importance of dissociation in the past. If survivors had no help or support, dissociation was probably a lifesaver for them. The problem is that dissociation takes on a life of its own. If it had been the main coping tool as a child, it may remain so for an adult unless a person works to change that. The change is important because rather than providing protection today, dissociation can put people at risk and interfere with decision making.

Keep in mind that the goal is to exchange one form of coping for another. Dissociation, numbing, and avoidance need to be exchanged for self-regulation. This exchange will help you to function more effectively *and* have protective coping strategies that don't restrict your life the way that traumatic stress responses do. Everyone needs defenses; the key is to be able to choose when you need them and how you will use them. With dissociation and numbing, there is no choice, no control. With self-regulation, you can determine what you need and how to manage things rather than being controlled by forces inside of you. It's the difference between having an instant, nearly automatic reaction and being able to choose your response.

On the next page is a quiz that you can take to see if dissociation really keeps you safe, or if it just gives the impression of safety without actually protecting you from harm. People usually have some strong beliefs about why they have to keep dissociating. You can address these beliefs and see if they still apply today.

Tool: Reality Check

Risks when Dissociative

To assess the effects of dissociation in your life, answer *yes* or *no* to the following:

When you dissociate or numb out these days, are you more likely to:

1. Hurt yourself?

yes   no

2. Get into a dangerous situation?

yes   no

3. Have more flashbacks?

yes   no

4. Lose track of who you are?

yes   no

5. Lose track of where you are?

yes   no

6. Feel frightened and vulnerable?

yes   no

What do you think of your answers? Do they surprise you?

_____

_____

_____

_____

Do you have mixed feelings about trying new ways of coping? If so, what are they?

_____

_____

_____

_____

Tool: Reality Check

Tool: Imagery

Goals: To reduce the frequency and intensity of unpleasant or frightening imagery and increase the use and effectiveness of positive, comforting, and helpful imagery.

Ideas:

Imagery is the result of the process of using your imagination. You can use your imagination to soothe yourself, to solve a problem, or to visualize a goal. However, your imagination can also frighten and confuse you when you think about scary things or picture frightening images. Traumatic stress responses and dissociative experiences often emerge through imagery that is unconsciously driven. In other words, you may not have control over it yet. You might sometimes scare yourself by imagining threats, negative outcomes, or other frightening things. When your imagination scares you, you may think that someone dangerous (from the past) is around. It is possible even to "see" that person. When people are under a great deal of stress, their imaginations can act as a movie projector, making them see scary or traumatic things that aren't happening in the present. With PTSD, a person's memory can call to mind frightening thoughts, pictures, sounds, tastes, smells and/or physical experiences from the past without even meaning to do so. These flashbacks are coming from the mind, so you need to use your mind—your imagination—to fight them and get them under control. It may be hard sometimes, to let yourself imagine "good" or positive things, especially if you believe that you don't deserve it. Fight those thoughts with everything that you have. They are part of the lies you were told. They are just another way for the past to hold you. Imagining makes things real. What do you want to be real?

Safe Places are images or pictures in your mind that are soothing or comforting. Safe place images can make you feel safer, more secure. Safe Places can be real or imaginary.

Imagery—using your imagination to manage stress responses and feelings.

Safe Places—real or imaginary places that you can visualize in order to feel safer, calmer, or to take a break from intense thoughts, feelings, or impulses.

Tool: Imagery

Imagery Worksheet 1

Recall a time or place where you felt loved, comfortable, secure or confident.
Where were you? (Inside? Outside? At home? On vacation?)

_____

What were you doing? What was going on?

_____

_____

Who was there? (Friends? Family? Pets?)

_____

What good feelings were you having that day? (Excitement? Satisfaction? Joy? Awe? Gratitude?)

_____

_____

Focus on those feelings for a moment. Imagine that you have a volume dial inside. Turn the feelings up a little as you slowly breathe deeply. Focus on every detail of the image of that day. Hold those feelings for a few minutes longer. Then, when you are ready, use the dial to turn them down. Allow the feelings to fade naturally. Try not to shut them off. Use the lines below to say something about the day that you pictured.

_____

_____

_____

You can use the space below to draw the feelings associated with that day.

Tool: Imagery

When you are stressed, anxious, or frightened, the ability to create space within yourself can help you "take a break" from life's struggles. This can be done with imagery. Why else would people hang scenic pictures at home, stack trophies on shelves, and keep calendars of beaches at work? These things bring to mind pleasant imagery in the middle of a hard day and allow people to imagine—to picture—how they would feel if they were at the beach instead of knee deep in paper work, or how they felt when they won that trophy. This can provide very real relief. This kind of imagery can reduce stress and tension in anyone.

For example, maybe you would like a tree house or a field full of wildflowers all to yourself. Then, when you are having a hard time, you could think about the tree house or the field and allow yourself to imagine every detail about how that place could soothe and protect you. Pretty soon you may find that you feel a little better because you took "time out" to think about and "visit" your safe place. The Safe Places exercise allows you to take a break when you need one, no matter where you are or what you are doing.

Work to create safe places that will be useful to you no matter what your state of mind.

You may need several different kinds of safe or protective places. Don't forget to attend to all parts of yourself as well as all feelings inside. For example, you may want to use different safe places depending on how you feel. Be specific. Would plants or animals be there? Is it inside or outside? Is it real or imaginary? Is your safe/protected place warm or cool? What would you have there? Toys or food? Draw or make a collage (pictures cut from magazines and glued onto a larger paper) of your safe places. Invite all parts of your mind to participate.

Remember that some places are unsafe and are not valid safe places. These unsafe places include bars or other scary, potentially abusive environments. Beware of places with mostly good associations where a trauma did occur. You may need different safe places for different times, depending on your mood. Some people find that it helps to keep their safe places secret. It helps them feel safer.

Take some time now to create a safe place or two (or more!) using the following worksheets.

Allow yourself to create joy and wallow in it as often as possible! These exercises might make the difference for you.

Imagery Worksheet 2

Right now, off the top of your head, list some of the most beautiful or soothing places you've been or seen.

_____

_____

_____

_____

_____

Ideas for safe places:

| a beach | the mountains | castle on a cloud | a cozy room | a tree house | a fort |
| a private island | a field of flowers | a sailboat | a rainforest with a waterfall | | a rainbow |

_____

_____

_____

_____

_____

You can use the space below to draw or attach soothing pictures.

Imagery Worksheet 3

Safe Places 1

1. Name or describe a situation, place, object, or color that makes you feel safer, more protected, soothed, calmer, or less tense (e.g., hiking, time with friends, the color blue).

_____

_____

_____

_____

_____

2. Draw, sketch, or cut and paste a picture of that situation, place, object or color in the space below or on a separate sheet if you need more room.

3. Describe, in detail, all of the aspects of your picture that make the place safe for you (e.g., the privacy, the location, the protective devices, the feelings that go with the place).

_____

_____

_____

_____

_____

4. Using the same technique, take the time to create safe places for all parts of yourself and that you can use in any mood state. You may want to use the following pages for your safe places.

_____

_____

_____

_____

_____

Tool: Imagery

Safe Places 2

1. This safe place is for_____ (e.g., a certain part of you or for use when you are in a certain mood).

2. Name or describe the situation, place, object, or color that makes you feel safer, more protected, soothed, calmer, or less tense (e.g., hiking, time with friends, the color blue).

_____

_____

_____

_____

_____

3. Draw, sketch, or cut and paste a picture of that situation, place, object, or color in the space below.

4. Describe in detail, all of the aspects of your picture that make the place safe for you (e.g., the privacy, the location, the protective devices, the feelings that go with the place).

_____

_____

_____

_____

_____

_____

_____

 *Tool: Imagery*

Safe Places 3

1. This safe place is for_____ (e.g., a certain part of you or for use when you are in a certain mood).

2. Name or describe the situation, place, object or color that makes you feel safer, more protected, soothed, calmer or less tense (e.g., hiking, time with friends, the color blue).

_____

_____

_____

_____

_____

3. Draw, sketch, or cut and paste a picture of that situation, place, object or color in the space below.

4. Describe in detail, all of the aspects of your picture that make the place safe for you (e.g., the privacy, the location, the protective devices, the feelings that go with the place).

_____

_____

_____

_____

_____

Tool: Imagery

Safe Places 4

1. This safe place is for_____ (e.g., a certain part of you or for use when you are in a certain mood).

2. Name or describe the situation, place, object, or color that makes you feel safer, more protected, soothed, calmer, or less tenses (e.g., hiking, time with friends, the color blue).

_____

_____

_____

_____

_____

3. Draw, sketch, or cut and paste a picture of that situation, place, object, or color in the space below.

4. Describe in detail, all of the aspects of your picture that make the place safe for you (e.g., the privacy, the location, the protective devices, the feelings that go with the place).

_____

_____

_____

_____

_____

_____

 *Tool: Imagery*

Safe Places 5

1. This safe place is for_____ (e.g., a certain part of you or for use when you are in a certain mood).

2. Name or describe the situation, place, object, or color that makes you feel safer, more protected, soothed, calmer, or less tense (e.g., hiking, time with friends, the color blue).

_____

_____

_____

_____

_____

3. Draw, sketch, or cut and paste a picture of that situation, place, object, or color in the space below.

4. Describe in detail, all of the aspects of your picture that make the place safe for you (e.g., the privacy, the location, the protective devices, the feelings that go with the place).

_____

_____

_____

_____

_____

You can follow this format in your journal and create as many safe places as you need.

Tool: Imagery

Tool: Gauge

Remember that imagery provides a way of using your imagination to soothe yourself, to set and plan for goals, and to practice steps toward achieving goals. Safe places can help with the self-soothing, but you will need more tools to help you with your goal of increased self-awareness. The next few pages introduce tools that you can use to keep track of your thoughts, feelings, and impulses. These imagery techniques will help you to be more self-aware, and will probably lead to some discomfort since traumatic experiences may have led to habits of reduced self-awareness. The following tools will help you reduce the intensity of feelings to more tolerable levels.

Idea: The three main categories of images for addressing thoughts, feelings, and impulses are gauges, regulators, and containers. These images are tools that assist in the toleration and management of thoughts, feelings, and impulses.

● **Gauges**—an image, a picture, or visualization of something that measures intensity. A gauge will let you know if pressure is too high or too low. Gauges are used to predict danger or to determine how well something is functioning. Your gauge can be a meter with one or several dials that measure different things like:

- racing thoughts
- intrusive emotions
- dangerous impulses
- the need for help

These gauges can be used to let you know when you are in the "red" or Danger Zone. You could use them to see how close you are to acting on impulses.

This gauge could be used to monitor four different things at one time. Using this type of image, you can check on the intensity of thoughts, feelings, impulses, and safety.

Whatever images you use to gauge intensity, you need to make sure that you set aside time to practice checking in with yourself. Practice will help the technique to become second nature and to work more effectively when you are having trouble.

 Tool: Gauge

Imagery Worksheet 4

Add to the list of common images used to gauge how a person is doing inside:

speedometer   thermometer   pressure gauge   blood pressure cuff

gas gauge   volume dial   weather patterns (storm blowing in, calm, hazy)

scuba gauge   volcano   clock (1=low intensity, 12=high intensity)

colors (gray = numb, blue = sad, red = overwhelmed)

10 Point scale 1-2-3-4-5-6-7-8-9-10 (1= low, 10=high)

_____

_____

_____

_____

_____

In the space below, draw some of the images you added to the list.

Tool: Gauge

Imagery Worksheet 5

Gauges (thermometers, dials, speedometers, scales, etc.)
Identify and draw (or cut and paste) three different gauges you could use to monitor how you are doing inside. You may need a separate gauge for 1) thoughts, 2) feelings, and 3) impulses.

- Choose images that describe your internal states
- Do your thoughts race?
- Are your feelings like waves or colors?
- Include at least one image that will work for younger parts of yourself if you have them.
- Make sure the images you are using aren't scary

1. These gauges are for thoughts.

A.

B.

C.

 Tool: Gauge

2. These gauges are for feelings.

A.

B.

C.

3. These gauges are for impulses.

A.

B.

C.

Tool: Gauge

Tool: Regulator

Idea:

• **Regulator**—an image that helps you to control the intensity of internal states. Regulators help you to manage whatever you have measured with your gauge. Your regulator needs to be able to turn things both up and down so that you can increase *and* decrease feelings. This is important because feeling numb is a danger sign and feeling overwhelmed leads to impulsivity. Your regulator needs to work in both directions. You may need different regulators to manage different problems like the following:

- intense or numb feelings
- intrusive visual hallucinations
- racing thoughts

Your regulator might turn things down or dim them out; it might have a different effect on different problems. It's all up to you.

• This regulator is a dial that can be used to turn painful feelings down or to turn pleasant feelings up. You could use it to turn sounds down inside when it's too noisy or to dim out scary images.

• This image of a remote control device can be used to control intrusive sounds and images. You might want to "change channels" from flashback images to safe place images, or you may want to watch the reality channel. You could use this image to "mute" scary sounds that you hear in your head or to fast forward through flashbacks. You could turn the volume up or down.

Images commonly used for regulating thoughts, feelings and impulses:

gas pedal/brake	faucet	thermostat
volume dial	waterfalls	remote control

weather (gentle rain expresses sadness, cool breeze reduces anger)

_____

_____

_____

_____

_____

Practice

It is important to remember that whatever image you use to regulate intensity, you should set aside time to practice. Practice will help the tool to become second nature and will allow it to work more effectively when you are having trouble. It often helps to first practice turning pleasant feelings up and down. And don't forget to breathe! Sometimes tension can build when practicing or using new techniques. Focusing on your breathing may help you reduce tension and anxiety. Breathing is very basic and can help you to get centered.

Imagery Worksheet 6

ACTIVITIES

Regulators

Identify and draw (or cut and paste) three different regulators that you could use to monitor how you are doing inside. You may need a separate regulator for 1) thoughts, 2) feelings, and 3) impulses.

1. These regulators are for thoughts.

A.

B.

C.

 *Tool: Regulator*

2. These regulators are for feelings.

A.

B.

C.

3. These regulators are for impulses.

A.

B.

C.

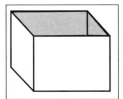

Tool: Container

Idea:

● **Containers**—provide a holding tank for intrusive, painful or disruptive thoughts, images, and feelings. A container will allow you to postpone working with something until you are ready. Containers work best when they seem to match your difficulty. If you are having intrusive pictures in your head, you might visualize a photo album that can be closed with the pictures inside. If your feelings are like floodwaters, you might need a strong dam with a spillway to contain them. Use your imagination. Different containers can be used for different problems. Scary intrusive images may be contained by using a TV, VCR, and remote control to stop the image, fast forward it, turn down the sound, turn the image off or eject the "tape" of the image.

● Racing thoughts can be contained by imagining they are on a radio; you can change the channel to soothing thoughts or a safe music station.

● Dangerous impulses could be contained in a safe with a time lock or a bank vault with safety deposit boxes

● Intense feelings could be contained in a dam with a spillway

Use the following worksheet to identify other useful containment images.

 Tool: Container

Imagery Worksheet 7

Add your ideas to the list of common images frequently used as containers:

Tupperware	hot air balloons	boxes	a safe with a time lock	photo album
scuba tanks	genie bottles	crates	vacuum cleaners	library
bank vaults	safe deposit boxes	bottles	computer disks	

_____

_____

_____

_____

In the space below, draw some of the images you have added to the list.

ACTIVITIES

Containers

Identify and draw (or cut and paste) three different containers you could use to hold intense feelings, thoughts, and impulses.

1. These containers are for thoughts.

A.

B.

C.

Tool: Container

Imagery Worksheet 8

2. These containers are for feelings.

A.

B.

C.

3. These containers are for impulses.

A.

B.

C.

 Tool: Container

Imagery Worksheet 9

Keeping Track Over Time

Practice checking in with yourself. Use your images. Use the chart below to keep track of periods of high and low intensity by first marking current intensity then goal intensity. To check in, stop what you are doing and focus on what you are thinking about, how your body feels, and how you are doing emotionally. Then notice how intense your thoughts, feelings and impulses are. Identify the feeling, and then rate its intensity on a scale of 1–10 and write the feeling and intensity in the table.

Examples: 1   2   3   4   5 ↑ 6   7   8   9   10 ↑

↑
(almost no feeling)   (moderately intense)   (overwhelming)

	Sunday	Monday	Tuesday	Wednesday	Thursday	Friday	Saturday
8:00 a.m.	Current: Sad –7, goal –4						

Feeling Chart (Use list from Appendix)

1   2   3   4   5 ↑ 6   7   8   9   10 ↑

↑
(almost no feeling)   (moderately intense)   (overwhelming)

	Sunday	Monday	Tuesday	Wednesday	Thursday	Friday	Saturday
8:00 a.m.							
9:00 a.m.							
10:00 a.m.							
11:00 a.m.							
12:00 p.m.							
1:00 p.m.							
2:00 p.m.							
3:00 p.m.							
4:00 p.m.							
5:00 p.m.							
6:00 p.m.							
7:00 p.m.							
8:00 p.m.							
9:00 p.m.							
10:00 p.m.							
11:00 p.m.							

Tool: Container

Do you notice any patterns related to your feelings and intensity? What are they? For example, some people don't notice their feelings except when they are extremely intense.

_____

_____

_____

_____

Are there certain times of the day when feelings get more intense? When? Why?

_____

_____

_____

Imagery Worksheet 10

Practice regulating the intensity of thoughts, feelings, and impulses by turning things up or down.

● Picture (or turn back to your drawing in Imagery Worksheet 6) your regulator and use it to turn down or reduce the intensity of your thoughts, feelings, or impulses. You can do this by picturing your gauge and noticing the intensity of your experience, and then slowly picturing the gauge changing as thoughts, feelings or impulses get smaller and smaller.

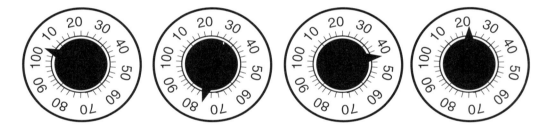

Each of these gauges represents a level of emotional intensity. You can put numbers around the gauges to show different levels of intensity. Use color-coding to show which levels of intensity are low, moderate, and high. Imagine feelings as they get stronger.

_____

Which levels can you tolerate without panicking?

_____

At which levels do you need help?

_____

From the imagery exercises you have completed, can you determine which tools help you tolerate feelings more effectively?

_____

 Tool: Container

Imagery Worksheet 11

Imagery does no good if you don't remember to use it. However, it can be hard to remember to do new things. **You need to practice reminding yourself that you have new tools.** You can remind yourself of this in many ways. Use self-talk or write notes to yourself. Practice using your tools on things that aren't upsetting. Picture or visualize a piece of fruit or a model of something, and then use imagery to make it more and less vivid. Use imagery to check in with small feelings. Don't wait until you are overwhelmed.

What can you do to *remember* to use imagery?

Example. Carry an index card on which you have listed techniques. Create an emergency kit in a small tin and keep pictures of soothing images inside of it.

_____

_____

_____

_____

_____

Just as professional athletes have discovered, practice will help you to use the skills when you need them the most. These skills may require a lot of practice and fine-tuning before they begin to work for you. Don't give up. The results are worth it!

Tool: Container

Tool: Journal Writing

Goals: To develop a habit of using a private journal for the purposes of grounding, developing safe places, reflecting, working internally, self-soothing, improving memory functioning, and documenting present-day experiences, thoughts, and feelings.

Ideas:

● **Journal**— It is incredibly important for all who are working on trauma recovery to use a journal. There are several reasons for this. A journal serves as a road map, a support, and a method of internal communication and self-expression. A journal is also a container. It is a powerful tool for people working on self-understanding and acceptance. You will definitely need a journal to use this handbook the way it is meant to be used. If you don't have one, make or get one! Make sure you get or make a journal that you like. Some people use tape recorders instead of a written journal. Use what works for you.

● **Level I**— Surface level; write about events of the day in a present-focused way. Don't write about feelings at this level. For journal writing to be safe and effective, it will help you to define different types of writing and to use structure when writing. Structure will help reduce the likelihood of becoming overwhelmed or frightened by your writings. Level I helps with grounding and managing time loss; complete sentences and spelling are *not* important. Work up to doing this kind of journal writing three times a day for up to five minutes each time. This kind of writing will help you become more aware of time loss. It will also put you in touch with the small positive or neutral things that happen each day. Noticing more about your day will help you to challenge negative thoughts. Do not judge what you are writing. This is an observation exercise. Try to stick to the facts.

● **Level II**— Present-focused. Write about feelings, thoughts, or impulses (urges), and about how your stress responses are affecting you. Use this level to vent and to work on internal awareness or communication. Use it to contain the feelings that come up that are too big to handle, and write about what you can handle. Use Level II to create or practice using safe places, self-soothing, or to work on therapy homework. Work up to doing this kind of journal writing at least twice a day for 10–15 minutes. Level II will help you to reduce intrusive thoughts, feelings, images, impulses, and internal interferences. You can set aside specific times to work on what you are thinking and feeling instead of ignoring those things. You may find that devoting a little time to yourself on a regular basis helps you to feel less overwhelmed each day. If this type of work brings up too much emotion and leads to dissociation or avoidance, go back to writing at Level I to get grounded.

● **Level III**— *Level III writng is not recommended unless you have therapy support. Writing about traumatic experiences is frequently de-stabilizing even with the help of an experienced therapist. Level III writing must always be used carefully and cautiously.* Present-focused work on traumatic material; to be used with professional therapy; writing about things you *remember* with the thoughts and feelings you had at that time. NEVER TRY TO "DIG UP" MATERIAL!!! This type of writing is best used sparingly. It can help you to connect thoughts and feelings from the past in order to understand your present difficulties. However, this kind of journal writing can really stir you up. If you aren't able to ground yourself very much, you should avoid this type of writing until you are more grounded. If you are doing this kind of journal writing and begin to lose track of reality, **STOP** and use self-regulation and grounding. Use this level carefully and for short periods of time.

As a rule, start with Level I and practice it until you can do it without slipping into other, more intense kinds of journal writing. Next, practice Level II in the same way. Use both together to practice grounding and self-regulation. **DO NOT** use Level III unless you can reliably and consistently use Levels I and II. No one should do trauma work without the basics of grounding and self-regulation. Also, try to limit journal writing to no more than 15 minutes at a time. This will help you to stay focused without getting as lost or overwhelmed. If you need to, set a timer so you will know when to stop.

Tool: Journal Writing

Journal Worksheet 1

On the lines below, write a brief description of your day so far. Use the guidelines for Level I writing from page 66. Write about events of the day in a present-focused way. Don't write about feelings at this level.

Example: *Slept about four hours last night, ate breakfast at 9 a.m., zoned out and found myself at work at 11 a.m.*

_____

_____

_____

_____

_____

_____

_____

_____

_____

_____

_____

_____

_____

_____

_____

_____

_____

_____

_____

_____

_____

_____

_____

_____

_____

_____

_____

_____

_____

_____

_____

_____

_____

Tool: Journal Writing

Journal Worksheet 2

On the lines below, write a brief description of your feelings right now. Use the guidelines for Level II writing. Write about feelings, thoughts, or impulses (urges), and about how your stress responses are affecting you.

Example: *Had rough day, felt weird, very sad, drew some of the sadness in my artbook, felt impulsive but didn't act on impulses to break things, called my friend for support.*

_____

_____

_____

_____

_____

_____

_____

_____

_____

_____

_____

_____

_____

_____

_____

_____

_____

_____

_____

_____

_____

_____

_____

_____

_____

_____

_____

_____

_____

_____

_____

_____

 Tool: Journal Writing

Journal Worksheet 3

This kind of writing often takes people closer to memories of trauma. It must be used carefully. Below are some examples of ways you could begin to write about traumatic experiences without being too graphic. Remember to limit the amount of time or space in the journal when you do this kind of writing. Allow yourself to work slowly. Beware of getting caught in the writing and being unable to stop. Set a timer if you think you might have trouble stopping. Plan to call someone if you need support before, during, or after using your journal.

Examples:

I remember being left alone and feeling scared. I thought I had done something wrong.

I had to hide in the closet to keep safe, but the darkness of the closet made me scared.

I never knew what I had done to make her so mad, but I always knew it was my fault.

She would trick me, make me think she was going to be nice. But she was always mean.

I get a lot of pain in my body when I think of those days. It's better than the pain in my heart.

Tool: Journal Writing

Techniques

1. *Dominant vs. non-dominant journal writing*—refers to using the hand you use most (dominant) vs. using the hand you use least (non-dominant). If you find yourself holding back too much or having trouble getting to feelings, switch hands. Ask questions with one hand and answer with the other.

2. *Clustering*—Begin with a central feeling or thought. Put that item in the middle of a page. Then, as quickly as you can, write whatever comes to mind in connection with that feeling or thought. Try not to censor yourself.

This cluster shows some of the feelings connected with anger. Sometimes this kind of writing is less threatening or less pressuring than writing out sentences can be. Look at what you have written. Write a bit more about the connections you have shown.

Example: *My angry feelings are connected to other feelings that I have. Sometimes they connect with my sadness and loneliness. Other times they connect with rage, depression, or fear.*

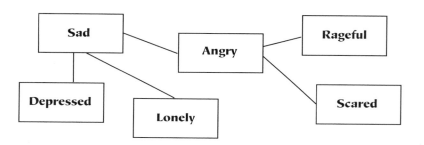

3. *Sentence stems*—these are used to help with journal writing when you might feel stuck.

For example:

When I am alone I think of . . .

When I am in a group I try to . . .

Usually my feelings are . . .

Keep a list of sentence stems in the back of your journal, and turn to them when you don't know what to write.

4. *Confidential journal writing*—sometimes you (or a part of you) may need to "get something out," but you really aren't ready to deal with that

material. In these cases, you can make a commitment with your self (selves) to write what you need to without reading it. You can fold the page over and agree not to read it right away, or show it to your therapist. This can meet the need to "get it out" and the need to contain (postpone addressing the issue) at the same time. Remember to go back to the issue later when it is safer.

5. *The five-minute sprint* is a technique that helps when you're stuck. Set a timer and write whatever comes to mind for five minutes nonstop. If you want to, you can write for a longer period of time, but as a rule, write for short periods of time to stay grounded.

6. *Simple or complex poems* can help people express themselves and are useful contributions to journal writing. Remember that it doesn't have to rhyme to be a poem!

Example:

"It is raining today, and that's how I feel, but not how I look. I look like a faded cloud that wishes it could rain."

Even a small poem can express a lot.

These are a few examples of journal-writing techniques. I recommend *The Way of the Journal* by Kathleen Adams (available through The Sidran Bookshelf) as a more complete journal reference and technique book.

Journal Worksheet 4

1. Use the space below to write vividly about a pleasant or enjoyable experience you have had. Be as descriptive as possible. Just write about the facts. Don't include feelings, and don't judge! Include a drawing or photograph if you want to.

_____

_____

_____

_____

_____

_____

_____

_____

_____

_____

_____

_____

_____

_____

2. Now list the feelings you had during that experience.

_____

_____

_____

_____

_____

_____

_____

_____

_____

_____

_____

_____

_____

_____

_____

Tool: Journal Writing

Journal Worksheet 5

1. Take three minutes (set a timer if you have one) to write about what you can observe going on around you right now. Be descriptive but nonjudgmental.

_____

_____

_____

_____

_____

_____

_____

_____

_____

_____

_____

_____

_____

_____

_____

2. List any feelings you notice about what you just wrote.

_____

_____

_____

_____

_____

_____

_____

_____

_____

_____

_____

_____

_____

_____

_____

Tool: Journal Writing

Journal Worksheet 6

1. Write about something you admire about yourself. Describe the qualities you admire most within yourself. Be specific about what these qualities mean to you.

_____

_____

_____

_____

_____

_____

_____

_____

_____

_____

_____

_____

_____

2. Write about the different aspects of your life that put you in touch with the qualities listed above. When do you notice those qualities?

_____

_____

_____

_____

_____

_____

_____

_____

_____

_____

_____

_____

_____

_____

_____

_____

 Tool: Journal Writing

Journal Worksheet 7

1. Write about someone you admire. Describe the qualities you admire most.

_____

_____

_____

_____

_____

_____

_____

_____

_____

_____

2. Does the person have qualities that you would like to develop? Identify one or two and say something about how you know they have those qualities.

_____

_____

_____

_____

_____

_____

_____

_____

_____

_____

3. Are there steps you could take to practice those qualities in the coming week? What are they?

_____

_____

_____

_____

_____

_____

_____

_____

_____

Tool: Journal Writing

Journal Worksheet 8

1. Write an alpha poem about a feeling you are having. An alpha poem is a poem written using the letters of a word on which you choose to focus.

Example: Write the word down the side of the page and then use the letters to write your poem

Sometimes **M**aybe
All I want to   or   **A**nger
Do is cry. **D**oesn't have to be violent.

_____

_____

_____

_____

_____

_____

_____

_____

_____

_____

_____

_____

_____

_____

_____

_____

_____

_____

_____

_____

_____

_____

_____

_____

_____

_____

_____

_____

Tool: Journal Writing

Journal Worksheet 9

1. Identify a decision you have to make over the next two days. Make a list of advantages and disadvantages about your choices.

Advantages	Disadvantages

2. List the feelings you have about the advantages and disadvantages.

_____

_____

_____

_____

_____

_____

_____

3. What are some reasons you might not want to look at advantages and disadvantages?
Example. I don't want to think about those things. Choosing is too hard.

_____

_____

_____

_____

_____

_____

4. How can you use your journal to help with making decisions?

_____

_____

_____

_____

_____

_____

_____

_____

Tool: Journal Writing

Tool: Safety

Goals: to define safety, to show the importance of safety, and to provide tools for the development of a comprehensive safety plan.

Ideas:

Safety means being reasonably free from harm or the immediate threat of harm regarding five boundary/need areas (emotional, spiritual, psychological, physical, and sexual).

Boundaries and safety are related issues. It is important to understand how they are related so that you can begin to see how they affect each other. Boundaries and safety are closely related to power and self-esteem.

Crash Course in Boundary Development

Power—In an average, "good enough" upbringing, babies learn about power through power sharing. A baby cries and gets fed, changed, held, and so on. If power is shared, a baby learns to trust and discovers that he or she can affect the world. At this stage, a child begins to learn about *hope.* If power isn't shared, the baby may learn mistrust and give up from hopelessness.

Self-Esteem—Average two- to three-year-olds are full of themselves and believe they affect every aspect of the world around them. If allowed to express themselves and to develop some independence (autonomy), they learn that they are valuable, a factor which increases self-esteem. At this stage, the child is working on a sense of *will.* If he or she does not feel self-esteem, their powerlessness gets stronger and they learn to doubt their worth and to feel ashamed and helpless.

Boundaries—Around the ages of 3 to 5, children begin to learn about limits, ownership, and other aspects of relationships. They begin to understand how things are separate and/or related. Children begin to want privacy and work on setting limits as well as to respond to limits being set. If there are no limits, children may either run wild or try to make limits in their minds in order to feel safe (e.g., fitting things into categories of good and bad, deciding that nothing is safe, or limiting almost everything to avoid finding out what's unsafe). At this stage, children work on taking the initiative and building confidence. They are developing a sense of *purpose.* In the absence of boundaries, a child may learn that there is no point to setting limits, because they get hurt anyway.

Safety—Ages 6 and up, children learn more about safety. They learn to avoid the stove not just because they'll get into trouble, but because it's dan-

Power—a sense of connectedness to your own ability to manage and direct your life (not to be confused with power over others).

Self-esteem—a sense of your own worth or value.

Boundaries—limits in relationships. Boundary areas are physical, sexual, emotional, psychological, and spiritual.

Safety—freedom or reasonable freedom from threat of harm to any of the five boundary areas.

Tool: Safety

gerous. Children with good boundaries view the world as basically friendly with some danger and untrustworthy people along the way, and this becomes a part of their identity. They are more confident and proud about their efforts and learn to feel *competent*. Children who have not been allowed boundaries may not recognize them and may feel rejected by others who uphold boundaries, or they might continually violate others' boundaries. Nothing feels safe, resulting in a deep sense of inferiority.

It is clear that chaos, deprivation, and abuses early in life seriously interfere with self-esteem, boundaries, and safety. How do you build or rebuild those parts of yourself? Well, self-help books talk about all kinds of ways of getting "empowered." The problem with instant empowerment is this: if you've never known power in your life or the ability to decide what happens to you, you cannot become *empowered* by a sheer force of will. So, do not despair if self-help hasn't worked for you. It may not be the best way to get in touch with your internal power source.

Some survivors have despaired because they consider themselves self-help failures. If you have found self-help to be inadequate, you have found out that you can't begin rebuilding your sense of self with power. You have to start with safety and work backwards. This may be a better method. In order to be safe, you must make safety your goal. You cannot expect anyone to keep you safer than you keep yourself. The responsibility is now yours.

Perceived and Actual Safety—There are two kinds of safety, perceived and actual. Perceived safety is how safe you *feel*. Actual safety is how safe you *are*. Traumatic stress responses and dissociation have the effect of confusing safety so that your feelings of safety may not be based on the reality of safety.

Very Unsafe 1 – – – – – – – – – – – – – – – – – – Very Safe 10	Perceived Safety	Actual Safety
Stress Responses	2	9
Dissociation	9	2

Stress responses and PTSD cause experiences that make you feel unsafe even when you may be under no threat of danger. Dissociation and numbing can make you feel perfectly safe, when in reality they rob you of awareness and make you more of a sitting duck! The trick is to recognize when feelings do and do not reflect reality. If you practice grounding and work to

Tool: safety

increase self-awareness, you will be more effective when it comes to knowing when you are safe and when you really are at risk.

Commitment to Safety—Perhaps safety is a daily or even a constant struggle for you. It is important to make safety the primary goal. The first step in being safe is to commit to doing your very best to stay safe, and when you cannot do it on your own, you should commit to calling and waiting for help. Then, you have to accept the help! Without this commitment to safety, recovery can be sidetracked by an endless succession of safety problems. Of course, sometimes it's more familiar to struggle with safety than it is to work on feelings. If you spend a lot of your time struggling with safety, you may want to ask yourself whether dangerousness is a method of avoiding something else that is painful or scary inside.

A Word About Addiction

Safety is a tricky subject. It has many meanings and differs depending on who you talk to. Trauma can lead to all kinds of addictions. Some people use drugs, some use alcohol. Some abuse prescriptions. Some people are *addicted* to chaos or crisis. They feel anxious when things are calm. Some people are addicted to self-harmful behavior or the adrenaline *rush* that comes with the fight-or-flight response. It is important to understand how addiction and traumatic stress can be closely intertwined. They connect with and can even trigger each other. In other words, using substances and other addictive behaviors can lead to flashbacks or more traumatic experiences. More flashbacks and more traumatic experiences can lead to a greater need to use substances or to other addictive behaviors. Beware of this cycle. Survivors caught in this cycle can become ever more desperate for the ultimate "relief" of suicide.

Tool: Safety

Safety Worksheet 1

1. Identify clues within yourself that predict dangerous or impulsive behavior (e.g., you isolate yourself, etc.).

_____

_____

_____

_____

_____

_____

_____

_____

_____

_____

2. Identify patterns of dangerousness (e.g., certain feelings typically leading to certain impulses—"When I am lonely, I usually want to go drink at a local bar or buy razor blades").

_____

_____

_____

_____

_____

_____

_____

_____

_____

_____

_____

3. Identify activities you could use to prevent yourself from acting on dangerous impulses.

IMPULSE	INTERVENTION
1. Hide in a corner	Use safe places to reduce fear
2. Punch wall	Take brisk walk around block (not at 4 a.m.!)
3.	
4.	
5.	
6.	
7.	

Tool: Safety

Safety Worksheet 2

While you are doing the safe activity, work on the things that may have upset you. Ask yourself these questions.

1. What were you thinking about before you became impulsive?

_____

_____

_____

_____

_____

_____

2. What were you feeling before you became impulsive?

_____

_____

_____

_____

_____

3. What has your day been like? Did anything upsetting happen earlier?

_____

_____

_____

_____

_____

4. Are there feelings you're trying to get rid of, avoid, or ignore?

_____

_____

_____

_____

_____

5. Can you turn a feeling down using imagery? Use the space below to show the feeling being contained or getting small enough to manage safely.

_____

_____

_____

_____

_____

 Tool: Safety

Safety Worksheet 3

1. After releasing some energy in a safe way (through a brisk walk, gardening, etc.), use artwork to express the feeling. (Do not draw behaviors; instead, draw feelings. Use colors and shading to show intensity of feelings.)

2. Write about the thoughts and feelings you are having, and then leave them in the space below. Afterwards, do something calming or uplifting. It's not enough to get rid of the impulses and avoid the behaviors. It is also important to address what led up to them or they will come back with greater strength. Fill the empty space inside with something healthy, life-affirming, or at least neutral. Be sure to keep your intervention list close at hand. You may need to copy it and keep it in several places.

Tool: safety

Safety Worksheet 4

Do you have a safety agreement with yourself, your therapist, or someone else? You may need one. When a person has grown up with constant danger, safety is a foreign idea and must be worked on daily. What a safety agreement can do for you is to remind you of your goal—**safety!** Your agreement does not have to be in writing, but writing it down can help. Sometimes just the act of reading your agreement can be enough to help you stay safe. Here is a sample agreement:

> *"I, and all parts of my mind, known and unknown, promise to do my (our) very best to stay safe, and when I (we) cannot do it on my (our) own, I (we) will call and wait for help and accept the help that is offered without acting unsafely. There are **no loopholes** in this agreement."*

Now, define your "very best"! Your "very best" means avoiding dangerous persons, places, and things, staying clean and sober, and working to be self-aware and recognize difficulties that are developing so that you can intervene in a timely way. Your "very best" means *no slacking!* You can't abandon safety because you are angry. You can't let go of responsibility because you're tired. Your "very best" means doing everything you can to promote your health and well being. That's a tall order, but even though it's your responsibility today, you can get help with it and develop allies and support systems.

_____

_____

_____

_____

Tool: Safety

What Is a Safety Plan?

In order to meet the goal to be safe, you need a thorough safety plan. A safety plan will be the tool you use to help you "do your very best to stay safe." It will help you to focus on your commitment and will help you to remember your resources. A safety plan is proof that you take safety seriously. In the same way that fire drills help people to practice fire safety and escape routes, you will need to practice safety drills so that you will be able to use your plans in a crisis, no matter how you are feeling. Safety requires that you pay attention to yourself and to the environment. You need to be able to recognize signs of risk and danger. Recognition of risk and danger leads to a choice about how you will proceed. You may take a calculated risk or none at all. In any case, environmental and self-awareness are the keys to safety. You need to ask yourself, "What signs exist inside of me that can let me know that I am less safe?"

Creating Your Safety Plan

Observe yourself in order to pick up on warning signs from within. When you notice one, write it in your plan in the section on stress responses/red flags on page 87. List your daily activities ahead of time. Don't wait until you are in crisis. It's too hard to think. Make sure your daily list includes time for journal writing, imagery, safe places, self-soothing, work, play, artwork, internal work. Doing all of these things on a routine basis will help you feel less out of control and overwhelmed.

Use the Worksheet on the Next Page to Create a Safety Plan

List your *crisis-management* activities ahead of time. Be sure to include phone calls to hotlines, safe use of prescribed medication, substitute activities, and emergency procedures.

Safety Worksheet 5

1. Make a list of the people in your life that you can count on in a crisis; include phone numbers (include friends, therapists, sponsors, and hotlines).

A_____

B_____

C_____

D_____

2. Safety is one of those things that is best managed in a preventive way. What preventive measures can you take to promote safety in general in your life? (*Examples:* Write in a journal daily, don't travel to unsafe parts of town, avoid associating with dangerous people.)

_____

_____

_____

3. Identify some natural consequences to unsafe behavior. (*Examples:* New scars, loss of friends, lower self-esteem)

_____

_____

_____

_____

4. Identify the steps you are willing to take to re-establish safety if you *do* behave in an unsafe manner or find yourself in an unsafe situation. (*Example:* Call for help)

_____

_____

_____

_____

5. What kinds of unsafe behaviors or situations are most tempting or difficult for you to avoid? (*Example:* Getting involved in relationships before you are ready.)

_____

_____

_____

_____

6. What are you willing to do to begin addressing these temptations in a healthy, helpful way?

_____

_____

_____

 Tool: Safety

Safety Worksheet 6–The Safety Plan

Daily Activities to Promote Safety	Stress Responses / Red Flags	Activities for Stress responses
Example: Practice grounding techniques 1st thing in the morning and before bed	Feeling hazy, disconnected, out of it, not able to concentrate, zoning out more	Name 5 things I see in the present, 5 things I hear, 5 things I feel (physically)
Check in with feelings three times a day	Staying in bed, not answering the phone	Write about feelings in journal, turn down intensity

Safety Contract

1. If you are ready to do it, write your own safety agreement below. Don't forget to sign it.

_____

_____

_____

_____

_____

_____

_____

There are no loopholes in this contract.

Signed,

Tool: Safety

Relaxation—tension- or stress-reduction.

Tool: Relaxation

Goals: To learn safe methods of tension reduction and relaxation in order to combat PTSD and numbing experiences and responses.

Ideas:

● **Relaxation** is the opposite of tension. Relaxation techniques may be thought of as techniques that make you feel less tense or less stressed. However, as strange as it may seem, relaxation takes effort. As you begin working on these exercises, keep in mind that they may seem foreign or even unnatural. That's your stress response talking. Remember to tell yourself that it is safe to practice relaxation at certain times and places. It is, in fact, necessary if you plan to be effective in other parts of your life. Too much stress ultimately works against you and can sap your energy, disabling you physically, emotionally or mentally. The goal, however, is not *complete* relaxation. Rather, it is *increased* relaxation.

● There are three primary types of relaxation:
1. *Physical*—dealing with the body; muscles and joints
2. *Mental*—dealing with the mind; thought processes and problem solving
3. *Psychological*—dealing with emotional conflict; overwhelming or painful feelings

● High levels of tension or stress in any of the above areas can influence stress in the others. In the same way, practicing relaxation techniques can reduce overall tension. Consider for a moment that you probably already use stress reduction in your life. Are you aware of the things that you do to reduce stress? For example, some people drink alcohol, use drugs, harm themselves, become violent, overeat, starve themselves, overspend, or have unsafe sexual encounters to relieve stress. While these things may relieve stress in one area, they usually lead to increased stress in other areas.

● *Physical* stress shows itself in many ways. You may notice tension headaches or even migraines, muscle or joint pain/soreness, stomach ailments, and similar physical problems.

● *Mental* stress shows itself in poor concentration, preoccupation with stressful thoughts, poor problem solving, and frequent errors in judgment.

● *Psychological* stress comes with internal conflict, mixed emotions, mood changes or struggles you experience within yourself.

Tool: Relaxation

The effort to reduce stress is often related to getting rid of painful feelings/emotions. Those emotions may frequently arise in relation to your thoughts.

For example:

R. doesn't have enough money to pay his electric bill this month. He feels nervous and worried. He thinks that it's disgraceful not to be able to pay his basic bills and fears that he will lose his electricity. He feels ashamed and angry with himself for the money problems he has. R. can't stand feeling angry. It makes him feel like a time bomb. He tears up the bill in anger and takes some sleeping pills to numb out. The anger is usually gone when he wakes up.

In this example, R. takes the pills to relieve the stress of his *anger*. He does nothing to relieve the stress of his *bill*. The anger has created a detour, and he is no longer focused on his bill. R. has reduced his ability to problem-solve. He may even forget about the bill. R. could benefit from some tension reduction/relaxation techniques. The relaxation could help him to focus on the problem in a calmer manner. Being calmer will allow him to reduce the stress of managing finances. Relaxation techniques and self-talk can help R. to manage his self-abusive thoughts. Those thoughts are the main source of his out-of-control anger. Reducing that anger can help him reduce his self-destructive behavior–abuse of sleeping pills.

Use the following relaxation worksheets and exercises to help reduce tension and increase problem-solving skills.

Tool: Relaxation

Relaxation Worksheet 1

Go for a 10-minute walk if weather permits, or listen to your favorite music for 10 minutes.
Do not continue with this worksheet until you have walked or listened.

Now that you have either walked or listened to music for 10 minutes, sit in a chair. Close your eyes. Think about how you felt, what you experienced.

A. Using the box below, draw a picture of your feelings. Use three colors.

B. Using the colors from your drawing, tell what they mean to you.

For example: *Gray* is the numbness I felt before listening to my music.
Red is the fear I feel when I don't feel numb.
Yellow is the warmth I feel when I am connected to music.

 Tool: Relaxation

Relaxation Worksheet 2

It can be helpful to think about relaxation existing on a continuum expressed through different shades of colors or the numbers 1–10. The continuum describes how tense or relaxed you are.

Red –Orange –Yellow –Green –Blue –Purple

Not at all relaxed 1—2—3—4—5—6—7—8—9—10 Very relaxed

(Very tense)   (Not at all tense)

1. Rate the level of tension you are having at this moment._____

2. Now, take a moment to become aware of your breathing. Just notice how you are breathing. Are your breaths shallow or deep?_____

3. If your breaths are deep, continue focusing on your breathing. Watch for long, slow, and deep breaths. If your breaths are shallow, focus on breathing from your abdomen. Your chest should not move very much, but your a domen should move. As you inhale, picture the oxygen moving deep into your lungs, then down to your abdomen. Then picture the air moving up through your abdomen, then through your lungs, then out as you exhale. If you are breathing from your abdomen, your waist should feel tight as you inhale, then relaxed as you exhale.

4. Continue to focus on breathing this way for a few minutes. It may seem like a long time. That's okay. It should.

5. Now, rate the level of tension you are feeling at this moment. _____

6. Is the rating different from the rating in #1? How so?

_____

_____

7. If the rating changed, why do you think it changed?

_____

_____

8. Did you notice that you were able to affect your level of tension/relaxation by what you focused on?

_____

9. List five things you think about that increase tension.

_____

_____

_____

_____

_____

10. List five things you can think about to reduce tension.

_____

_____

_____

_____

11. Go do one of the things you listed in number 10.

Tool: Relaxation

Relaxation Worksheet 3

When people use drugs, alcohol, aggression, violence, or self-harm to reduce stress, what other problems come up as a result?

_____

_____

_____

_____

_____

Do these other problems increase the need for stress reduction or increase stress in other areas of your life?

_____

_____

_____

_____

_____

What pattern do you notice in yourself regarding the use of unhealthy or self-destructive methods of stress reduction?

_____

_____

_____

_____

_____

Below is a list of safe, healthy alternatives to dangerous methods of stress reduction.

1. Deep breathing creates an immediate relaxation response at a cellular level (do it slowly)
2. Yoga or other low-impact stretching increases flexibility and relaxes the mind and body
3. Therapeutic massage
4. Reading (not horror or true crime!)
5. Music
6. Warm shower or bubble bath
7. Talking to either a friend or therapist (don't confuse the two)
8. Hobbies/Sports
9. Laughter

10. (Add your own here)

_____

_____

_____

 Tool: Relaxation

Identify specific techniques that will help you achieve a specific type of relaxation.

Mental Relaxation	Psychological Relaxation	Physical Relaxation

Ex. Pleasure reading	Ex. Safe places imagery	Ex. Play with a pet

Tool: Relaxation

Relaxation Worksheet 4

Try to take note of times when you feel relaxed. Add them to your list. In order to allow these techniques to work, you will have to take hold of your thoughts. This means that you have to focus your thoughts on things that calm and relax you. You must try not to think about things that increase anxiety when you are working on relaxation. If you practice this method, you'll be surprised at how you can control your thoughts and your level of tension.

List your top five anxiety producing thoughts or beliefs. (*Example:* "It'll never get better.")

1._____

2._____

3._____

4._____

5._____

List five calming thoughts. Don't try to fool yourself. Just list five calming thoughts that you actually believe. (*Example:* "I am learning about healing.")

1._____

2._____

3._____

4._____

5._____

At most, allow yourself ten minutes of heavy-duty worrying each day, and then practice turning your mind away from your worries toward other more productive thoughts. Has worrying benefited you in the past? Practice exchanging calming thoughts for anxiety-producing thoughts. Record the results in your journal. (You *do* have a journal, don't you? . . . just checking!)

Now, if you feel up to it, stand up. Go on, no one is watching. Hold your arms out at right angles from your body, straight out parallel to the ground. S-T-R-E-T-C-H! Do the same thing with your arms straight up in the air. Bring your arms back down to your sides, and shrug your shoulders up to your ears. Roll them back, and then let them drop gently. Lastly, wrap your arms around yourself and squeeze tightly. If it helps, think of what you are doing as a hug. If it doesn't, think of it as stretching your muscles in your back. To wrap up, shake your arms vigorously but *not* so it hurts! Shake out all of the negative junk you picked up today. Now sit and feel the relaxation. Write about the experience below or in your journal.

_____

_____

_____

_____

_____

_____

_____

_____

 Tool: Relaxation

Tool: Sleep Strategies

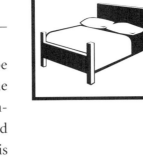

For people who have had traumatic experiences, sleep disturbances can be a serious problem. Sleep disturbances may include nightmares, nighttime flashbacks, difficulty falling or staying asleep, and early morning awakening. These disturbances can interfere with more than just sleep. The need to sleep is normally tied to the biological clock. The need for sleep is stronger at certain times of the day. Sleep is required in order for you to be able to think clearly during the day. Sleep helps to repair and restore the mind and body after your daily activities. Some of the repairs include digestion, removal of wastes, and restocking important chemicals in the brain. These are obviously essential activities. Sleep deprivation frequently causes dizziness, poor concentration, hand tremors, and hallucinations. Deprivation of dream sleep specifically can result in increased anxiety, irritability, and poor concentration. Clearly, sleep is an important part of healthy living.

Sleep patterns can differ in people with and without posttraumatic experiences, but the average adult sleep cycle is shown below.

Non-PTSD

The long spikes represent various stages of sleep, while the short spikes represent **REM** sleep or dream sleep. Normally, during about eight hours of sleep a person will cycle in and out of dream sleep several times. It is also normal to awaken during the night. REM/dream sleep has a curious effect when a person is sleep deprived. If someone misses a lot of REM/dream sleep, that person will have more REM/dream sleep the next time he or she falls asleep. This is called a rebound effect.

It is important to understand the rebound effect because avoiding sleep to avoid nightmares (occurring during REM sleep) increases the likelihood that you will have nightmares the next time you go to sleep. Your sleep pattern may look something like this:

PTSD

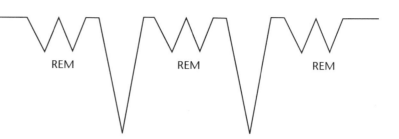

The long line represents wakefulness followed by increased REM sleep when you finally have fallen asleep. Since avoiding sleep doesn't seem to be the answer, what *is* the answer? Planful sleep strategies help those with PTSD to maximize sleep during the night when the body is most ready to sleep.

A complete sleep plan requires discipline and consistency. As you work to set up your plan, keep in mind that you want to create one that you will be able to follow most of the time. Review the last chapter, on relaxation. You will need to refer to it for your sleep plan. Getting enough sleep requires planning that starts in the morning. As you practice your sleep plan to get back to a regular pattern, avoid sleeping in and avoid naps. Naps can reset your internal clock and ruin your sleep at night.

General ideas:

DO . . .

eat regular, nutritious meals

exercise during the day

make your bedroom comfortable and soothing

leave a night-light on if you need to

go to bed at the same time each night (within ½ hour)

have some light reading material or picture books available

go to bed grounded!

have a light snack before bed (if you want)

Tool: Sleep Strategies

DON'T . . .

use alcohol or drugs that aren't prescribed to you

use caffeine (watch out for chocolate and sodas)

watch the news or disturbing TV shows

accept phone calls after a certain hour

stay on the Internet

read scary or troubling material (like bills!)

lie in bed worrying

take naps!

Tool: Sleep Strategies

Sleep Worksheet 1

1. Set a bedtime—If you usually fall asleep around 1:00 a.m., set your bedtime for 1:00 a.m. Don't try to go to bed at 9:00 p.m., or you might just lie awake. Set a reasonable bedtime based on your usual habits. You can always move it earlier or later as your sleep plan begins to take effect.

2. Set medication time—If you take medications at bedtime, talk with your doctor about how to make sure they are going to have the best chance of working for you. You don't want to take them too early, or they might wear off. Take them too late and you might be "hung over." The key is to take them in time to make you sleepy at your set bedtime. After taking your medications, the rest of the time needs to be spent trying to get sleepy.

3. Begin routine—
> **a.** hygiene—brush teeth, wash face, take warm bath or shower; *when* you choose to do these things depends on you and whether they wake you up or prepare you for sleep.
>
> **b.** relaxation—refer to the list you made in the last chapter; do things that relax you and allow your medicines to work, use "safe places"; if you have **DID**, tuck all parts of yourself in for the night; reassure yourself of your current history of safety in your room; play a relaxation tape or some soft music; leave a small light on if you need to.

4. Get in bed—Get into bed only if you feel sleepy. If you go to bed and can't sleep, get out of bed and go back to do your relaxation exercises. Jot down worrisome thoughts in your journal to be dealt with later (don't get into any heavy journal writing). Try the following exercise to fall asleep grounded:

Example:
> *"I am aware that I see the window."* Say this slowly, five times.
> (Say what you see in your room. You can say the same thing five times or say five different things.)
> *"I am aware that I hear the fan."* Say this slowly, five times.
> (You can say the same thing five times or say five different things.)
> *"I am aware that I feel my pillow."* Follow the format above.

Go through the whole process again, this time saying what you are aware of four times, then three, then two, and then one. Chances are, you will drift off before you finish. For obsessive types, it's okay not to finish! This will help you to fall asleep completely grounded. It's not a bad waking exercise either, especially if you feel anxious or panicked. If the above exercise feels too complicated, just read *Goodnight Moon* (by Margaret Wise Brown) at bedtime.

5. In case of nightmares—Get Up! Get Grounded! Don't just roll over. You might fall back into the nightmare. Keep a sign by your bed that tells you the month and year, letting you know you are safe. Practice the grounding/awareness exercise mentioned above. Once you are grounded, go back to the relaxation routine, and go back to bed when you feel grounded and sleepy. Sometimes it may help to jot down the general content of the nightmare as a way of containing it. Use your own judgment as to whether this is a good idea for you.

Remember that sleep disturbance is part of PTSD and may persist while symptoms are severe. The goal is to maximize your sleep.

 Tool: Sleep Strategies

Sleep Plan 1

Create a thorough sleep plan using this worksheet.

Bed time: _____

Medicine time:_____

Routine:

Hygiene: *brush teeth*

_____

_____

_____

_____

_____

_____

Relaxation: *cup of herbal or decaffeinated tea*

_____

_____

_____

_____

_____

_____

_____

In case of a nightmare . . .

Get up, turn on a light

Get grounded

Think of Safe places

_____

_____

_____

_____

_____

_____

In case you wake up to real danger or real noise outside from neighbors or other sources, don't forget to keep safe. Don't take any risks, and call for help if you need to. This type of plan should help you get more sleep, but you may still have problems. Do the plan above first. If it doesn't work, use these techniques with the plan on the next page faithfully for seven days, and you should see a clear improvement in your nighttime sleep.

Tool: Sleep Strategies

Sleep Plan 2

Combine the following plan with the self-soothing and relaxation techniques previously mentioned.

 1. Set your clock for 6:00 a.m.

2. Go to bed sometime after 9:00 p.m. when you can't keep your eyes open anymore.

 3. Get up at 6:00 a.m., shower, dress, and start your day . . .

4. Don't take any naps!

5. Go back to #1, setting your clock for 6:00 a.m.

This plan has been known to help reset the sleep cycle when used faithfully. If it fails you, please let me know! Remember, the more you customize your sleep plan to fit your life, the better it will work for you. Good luck, and remember, good sleep takes discipline and consistency.

 Tool: Sleep Strategies

What Does it all Mean?

The Meaning of Awareness

Webster's Dictionary defines the word *aware* as 1) watchful and 2) having or showing realization, perception, or knowledge. Awareness, then, means the condition of being watchful or of realizing, perceiving, or knowing. It is interesting to note that the two most extreme outcomes of trauma (especially in childhood) are excessive watchfulness (posttraumatic hypervigilance) and reduced access to knowledge (numbing/dissociation). The result is watchfulness without true awareness and ignorance without bliss. Ignorance is used in the true sense of the word: lacking information, being unaware. For trauma survivors who dissociate, it is very disturbing to have evidence of one's own behavior and no memory of having engaged in it.

Awareness is a two-edged sword for most survivors. A difficulty exists in that awareness is the cure for avoidance, yet awareness puts you in touch with thoughts, feelings and impulses that can be extremely distressing. Backing up to look at the big picture shows how awareness is necessary for reducing the effects of trauma on survivors. However, it is important to distinguish between awareness with self-regulation and flooding. Flooding is a natural phase of the trauma response in which a person is overcome by an intense awareness of a traumatic event. The person may experience huge waves of feelings all at once. Healing awareness is *not* the same as flooding, although it may feel like it at first. Also, awareness is *not* about delving into the past. Awareness is a present-focused activity (starting with grounding) requiring that you observe yourself and your environment in the moment.

Becoming more aware or mindful takes practice. The first step is to be willing. The next step is to begin to pay attention to thoughts, feelings, and impulses. In other words, you have to stop doing the things you've usually done to avoid thoughts, feelings and impulses. You probably have your own ways of distracting yourself. Awareness includes becoming aware of those distractions. Many people fear that increased self-awareness will lead to increased traumatic experiences, but that does not necessarily follow. One thing that you *can* be sure of is that increased awareness will help you to be more in touch with all kinds of experiences—whether pleasant, painful, or neutral.

The previous sections of this workbook were meant to prepare you to practice increasing self-awareness without flooding yourself. Remember to pace yourself as you work. Pacing can help reduce the likelihood of becoming flooded.

Awareness Worksheet 1

What might it mean for you to be more self-aware? Take a moment to check in with yourself.

What are your fears about increased awareness?

_____

_____

_____

_____

_____

_____

_____

What are your hopes or wishes about increased awareness?

_____

_____

_____

_____

_____

_____

_____

_____

What do you think will *really* happen if you increase your self-awareness?

_____

_____

_____

_____

_____

_____

_____

_____

If you have answered the questions on this page, you have increased your internal awareness. You took a moment to focus your mind, think about yourself, and communicate those thoughts. The process can be as simple as that. But while it may be simple, it isn't always easy. Be prepared for internal resistance to increased self-awareness. This is natural, so don't worry too much about it. Just continue to pace yourself and practice the skills in this book.

The Meaning of Awareness

Tool: Self-Awareness

Objectives:

To decrease fear of self-awareness, develop skills for becoming more self-aware, and provide practical uses of tools for enhancing safety and self-care.

As you know, traumatic experiences naturally prompt avoidance as a protective measure against overwhelming thoughts and feelings during a crisis. Yet avoidance can seriously interfere with your ability to keep track of what's going on inside. When a person can't keep track of what's going on inside, it becomes more difficult to keep track of what goes on *outside* too. While avoidance may have been helpful in the past when you probably had fewer resources and little support, it can lose its effectiveness in the present and can become disabling. When avoidance has been a way of life, increasing self-awareness can seem virtually impossible. Also, self-awareness can frequently be a painful process! Internal awareness provides access to hidden resources *and* hidden pain. Many people are willing to forego the resources in order to avoid the pain. The problem with that trade-off is that the pain comes up anyway, and without the resources, life can become unmanageable. Each of us must decide the costs and benefits of continuing in this way.

Traumatic stress adaptations that reduce internal awareness include the following:

1. numbing, emotionally or chemically
2. avoidance
3. limited ability to feel or express emotions.

Dissociative adaptations reducing internal awareness include these:

1. trance-inducing behavior/ self-hypnosis
2. switching (moving into different personality states)
3. time loss
4. amnesia
5. depersonalization (out of body experiences)
6. derealization (feeling in a dream-like state).

Tool: Self Awareness

Begin by looking at the differences between dissociation/avoidance/numbing and self-awareness.

Dissociation/Avoidance/Numbing	Self-Awareness
Being unaware of what's inside	Being aware of what's going on inside
Feeling safe but not being safe	Increasing safety through awareness of resources
Making problem solving hard	Increasing awareness of choices
Reducing self-control	Increasing self-control
Limited access to feelings	Providing access to feelings

Add any other differences you may have noticed yourself.

Dissociation/Avoidance/Numbing Reduces Awareness of Internal States.

The whole adaptive value of dissociation lies in the fact that it reduces your awareness of yourself during moments of overwhelming or traumatic stress. Dissociation allows you to do what needs to be done to survive without giving you present awareness of potentially debilitating feelings. As mentioned before, if dissociation, avoidance, and numbing are your main methods of coping, the result is a reduction in overall awareness, not just a reduction in awareness of painful thoughts and feelings. Reduced self-awareness can allow for the re-creation of sensations that were experienced during the original traumatic events. As you dissociate, avoid, or numb out in the present, you may be connecting with the memory pieces that were created during traumatic experiences. Those memories (stored as intense emotion and physical sensations) can erupt in the form of flashbacks. Therefore, reduced self-awareness today may actually contribute to traumatic stress reactions such as intrusive experiences and flashbacks later on.

Tool: Self Awareness

Dissociation/Avoidance/Numbing Can Make You Feel Safe Even when You're Not.

It is very important to understand that *feeling* safe and *being* safe are not the same thing. Similarly, feeling threatened and being threatened aren't the same. Dissociation, avoidance, and numbing provide a feeling of protection in present-day life without actually protecting you. Dissociation, avoidance, and numbing tell you that if you aren't aware of something, it does not affect you. The question is, when you dissociate, avoid, or numb out, are you truly shutting out threatening experiences or just postponing the experience? Flashbacks indicate that you must have taken in some part of the traumatic experience. You may have stored it in the unconscious only to have it replay like a horror movie when you least expect it. Today's dissociative experience can become tomorrow's flashback.

How Do Dissociation/Avoidance/Numbing Interfere with Problem Solving?

Dissociation, avoidance, and numbing take you out of the problem-solving loop! If you are not in touch with present-day reality, you can lose track of present resources and options. Dissociation, avoidance, and numbing can also make it hard for you to remember that you're an adult. This can lead to flashbacks and re-traumatizing experiences. Rather than responding in a present focused way, you may respond as you did in the past, which makes the flashback experience even stronger.

Dissociation/Avoidance/Numbing Interfere with Self-Control and Self-Regulation.

Dissociation, avoidance, and numbing reduce self-control because you have limited knowledge of what is going on inside. You do not recognize what your reactions and feelings are. This makes it harder to connect thoughts, feelings, and behaviors in meaningful ways. When things are that disconnected, it is harder to make healthy decisions, and a "quick fix" becomes more attractive. Besides, many people have reported that the disconnectedness makes them feel crazy. A "quick fix" may *seem* like a good way of handling intrusive thoughts, feelings, or other problematic experiences, but *is* it a good way in the long run? The truth is, there are some perfectly healthy quick fixes like safe places and distraction. You just have to know what you are choosing and why. The old quick fixes may *seem* more attractive than the new ones. Practice the new ones until they feel like second nature.

Tool: Self Awareness

Dissociation/Avoidance/Numbing Limit Access to Feelings

You may be thinking, "That's the whole point! Dissociation, avoidance, and numbing are supposed to limit access to feelings and memories. Feelings are painful and disruptive, not to mention dangerous!" Feelings may be painful and disruptive, but consider that your feelings provide information about how you are doing in relationship to someone or something else. Feelings provide data. Without them, you cannot know how you are doing. Dissociation, avoidance, and numbing protect you from awareness of feelings during crises, but over time they leave you numb and out of touch. You can no longer know how you are doing. You may not trust yourself and may stop feeling alive. A life without feelings is merely existence. Moving beyond survival means acknowledging a hunger for something more meaningful and fulfilling than existence. Feelings are part of the answer to that hunger.

 Tool: Self Awareness

Self-Awareness Worksheet 1

What are some of the quick fixes you use when you are very disconnected or are having posttraumatic experiences?

_____

_____

_____

_____

What are the potential benefits of using quick fixes?

_____

_____

Would you say that some of these quick fixes have consequences? If so, what are they?

_____

_____

_____

_____

What are the risks involved with using quick fixes?

_____

_____

_____

_____

Why or when do you choose the quick fix over a more long-term solution?

_____

_____

_____

_____

Be honest about your thoughts and feelings. Read over what you have written on Self-Awareness Worksheet 1, and write about or discuss your thoughts about your writing. Do your thoughts look different on paper?

_____

_____

_____

_____

_____

Sometimes quick fixes allow you to protect yourself until you get to a healthier solution. You can also develop healthy quick fixes to use on a regular basis. The key is to be able to *choose* the coping skill or solution that will work best in a given situation. Don't forget that the goal is to be able to tolerate and control the intensity of feelings, not to make them go away.

Tool: Self Awareness

Participant/Observer

Self-awareness is a process of both participating and observing. The idea is to notice what is going on inside, feel it, attend to it, and notice where it is taking you in your thoughts and feelings. This can help you to connect with your experiences and manage them more effectively. You don't have to like what you are noticing. Notice that you don't like it.

Example: *"I am noticing that I am feeling more tense. I am aware that I am feeling angry. I am noticing that it bothers me to feel angry, I have negative thoughts about it. I am aware of impulses to hurt myself to make the anger go away."*

Using language like "I am noticing" or "Isn't it interesting that I feel . . ." helps you to acknowledge what's going on but also allows some healthy distance to reduce the likelihood of your becoming overwhelmed. It is important for you to practice participant/observer language in order for it to be helpful in a crisis.

On the next few pages, you will look at some tables that can help you understand feelings, mood states, and personality changes. The tools may help you to work with yourself more effectively.

Tool: Self Awareness

Self-Awareness Worksheet 2

The next few pages focus on a table that can be used to help you increase awareness of the relationships among your thoughts, feelings, impulses and behaviors. Use the descriptions and questions on the following pages to help you complete the table on page 112. Look at the example below.

Feeling	Age	Thought	Impulse	Behaviour	Need	New Behavior
Sadness	12	Nobody cares; I'm all alone	Hide, hurt self; pick a fight	Isolate, hurt self	Guidance, help, Support, love	Call someone, use journal, do artwork

Feelings: In this box, write down a feeling you currently experience. Focus on feelings that are especially problematic for you. You may think that you don't have many feelings, but as you do this exercise you will probably notice that you feel many different emotions at different times or even at the same time.

Age: In this box focus on how old you feel when you are having the emotion. For example, when you feel sad, do you feel your actual age, or do you feel like an adolescent or a child? Sometimes different emotions may prompt you to feel young and vulnerable or adolescent and rebellious, and sometimes you may just feel like yourself. Use the age box to show how your feelings affect your perception of age, maturity, or development. If you have a history of childhood trauma, you may have noticed that certain feelings are sometimes linked to certain ages or developmental levels. Understanding this connection will help you make sense of your experience and the reasons that your self-perceptions can change according to how you feel.

Thoughts: In this box, write the thoughts that typically go through your head when you are feeling the emotion. This will help you recognize thought patterns associated with certain developmental stages and emotions. This is important because the way that you think has an impact on the way that you feel, and vice versa.

Impulses: In this box, note the urges that accompany the thoughts, feelings, and developmental age. *Frequently, impulses seem to come from out of nowhere, but in reality they often have traceable beginnings.* Impulses can start as an idea first. Connecting impulses to thoughts and feelings can help you predict when they are coming. You will be able to identify patterns in your life that lead to impulsivity. This will enable you to change those patterns.

Behavior: Write down the behaviors that you typically engage in when you are experiencing the feeling, thoughts, and impulses you have noted. Sometimes the behavior will be the same as the impulses, but this is not always the case.

Need: In this box, write down what you are needing when you are experiencing the feeling, thoughts, and impulses you have noted. In the example given in the table, you can see that feeling sad leads to feeling younger, more alone, and unsupported. These feelings prompt impulses to hide (as well as others) that may be followed by hiding or self-harm. When you feel sad, you may need attention and guidance; however, in the table's example, the behavior listed is not likely to help you get your needs met.

New Behavior: Write the kinds of *new* behaviors you can practice to increase the likelihood of getting your needs met. When you're having strong feelings, most of your needs may involve assistance in the context of a relationship of some kind, yet your behaviors may be isolative and alienating. New behaviors that help you reach out to helpful, healthy relationships are more likely to meet your needs. The more you practice the new behaviors, the less isolated and alone you will feel when you are sad.

Tool: Self Awareness

Feeling	Age	Thought	Impulse	Behavior	Need	New Behavior

 Tool: Self Awareness

Self-Awareness Worksheet 3

If you have an idea of what might help, what could keep you from doing it? The following questions can help you to explore barriers to increasing self-awareness.

1. I have to keep my feelings hidden from myself because if I don't _____
_____
_____

2. Feelings are only good for _____
_____
_____

3. My feelings frequently lead to _____
_____
_____

4. I can't afford to be direct about my needs because _____
_____
_____

5. I prefer old behaviors because _____
_____
_____

6. Do your old behaviors get your needs met? If not, why not? If so, how?
_____
_____
_____
_____
_____

7. Are the new behaviors *more* likely to get your needs met? If so, how so?
_____
_____
_____
_____
_____
_____
_____

Tool: Self Awareness

Self-Awareness Worksheet 4

For anyone with DID (dissociative identity disorder), the next few pages focus on a table that can be used to help you increase awareness of different aspects of your dissociated self/selves. Use the descriptions and questions to help you complete the table.

Begin by inviting all parts of yourself to help you complete the worksheet.

Name	Age	Likes	Dislikes	Job	Safe Place	Wants/Wishes
Jimmy	9	Legos, candy, reading, quiet	The dark, being in a crowd	Watch other kids	Tree house	Wants to feel safer inside

Name: Some people who have other parts inside have names for them. Others may refer to parts of themselves by age, feeling, behavior, or by a birth name. For example, a man named Ron with DID might refer to some parts as Ronnie, Ron-18 (as in 18 years old), or maybe even as the Sad One. Use the "Name" box in the diagram to express what you call different parts of yourself or the way you identify that part of you (maybe with a feeling word like Sadness).

NOTE: Be sure to avoid demeaning or hurtful labels like the Creep or the Loser. These kinds of labels decrease trust inside and are hurtful.

Age: In this box, write the age or developmental stage of that part of yourself. Maybe you don't know the age but you have a sense that he or she is a child or adolescent. You can always ask in your mind for a part of you to tell you his or her age. Including ages will help you understand that parts of your mind may be "stuck" or "trapped" at different developmental stages and may need age-appropriate help.

Likes: Invite parts of you to write in things that they like, such as music, pizza, coloring books, movies, and so on. Completing this section will tell you some things that you can do to begin nurturing your whole self.

Dislikes: Invite parts of you to write in things that they don't like, such as the dark, spinach, people who are angry all of the time, and so on. Completing this section will tell you what some of your triggers are and some of the fears that you may need to work on. This section can also help with self-nurturing as you work to pay attention to your needs inside.

Job: All parts of your mind have a job or role inside. Some parts are protective, some manage finances, and some may hold certain feelings. Ask all parts of yourself to let you know who is responsible for what inside, and write down the answers in this section.

Safe Place: If you completed the chapter on Imagery, you probably created safe places for all parts of yourself. If not, make creation of safe places a priority. Let all parts of yourself write where their safe places are. Follow the guidelines for safe places.

Wants/Wishes: This is a very special section that allows all parts of you to express some desires and dreams/wants and wishes. This section can tell you a lot about yourself and can help you to be more focused in your recovery.

As you can see, whatever you are able to understand about your internal world will help you to direct your life. The information you get from this chart can tell you a lot about yourself. For instance, "Jimmy" is too young to be responsible for other inside child parts. From what is in the chart, we can see some ways of beginning to nurture "Jimmy" by attending to his likes and dislikes and working to meet his needs. Even if you don't get much information at first, whatever you get will be useful at some point.

 Tool: Self Awareness

This chart will help witn internal communication if you have DID.

Name	Age	Likes	Dislikes	Job	Safe Place	Wants/Wishes

Tool: Self Awareness

Self-Awareness Worksheet 5

As you work on increasing internal awareness, you can expect to feel resistance inside. In other words, you may find yourself avoiding the exercises that promote awareness, like journal writing, internal self-talk, and so on. This is a normal part of learning about yourself and it needs to be explored. Often, resistance is part of an effort to defend against things that are unacceptable to us; we try to disown parts of ourselves because we don't like certain things about us. This can lead to all kinds of unsafe behavior. In order to be aware of your resistance to internal work, explore the following questions.

1. If I start paying attention to my internal world, I am afraid that _____

_____

_____

_____

_____

2. I have to keep things hidden and separate because _____

_____

_____

_____

3. If I start looking inward I might have to give up _____

_____

_____

_____

4. I have mixed feelings about increasing self-awareness. My mixed feelings include: _____

_____

_____

_____

5. I am willing to practice internal awareness by doing more _____

_____

_____

_____

_____

Remember that increasing internal awareness will expose you to *both* hidden resources and hidden pain; you can't have one without the other, but your resources will help you with the pain.

 Tool: Self Awareness

Tool: Boundaries

Objectives: to define and identify boundaries, and to clarify the relationship between boundaries and safety.

Concepts:

Boundaries define limits in relationships. Increasing internal awareness will put you in touch with thoughts and feelings about the different relationships you are in. Boundaries in interpersonal relationships define both limits of interaction and the nature of your relationships with other people. Boundaries give you the room to be yourself and to express yourself according to your experiences. They provide you with the defining area of who you are. In the absence of interpersonal boundaries, you are at risk of losing your sense of self as separate from but related to others. Boundaries may need to change as relationships change.

Boundaries are not about withholding. They are about freedom and responsibility in preserving relationships. Boundaries involve the effort to be an individual *separate from* but *related to* others. That means being close without being engulfed and getting distance without having to alienate. Your boundaries serve to define your differences as they affirm your relatedness. Some boundaries may be non-negotiable. Others may shift depending on situations.

One of the problems with boundary areas is that also represent areas of *need*. The practice of getting needs met at the expense of boundaries is a problem for many people, with or without a trauma history. Boundaries exist in relationships, and you are responsible for respecting your own boundaries as well as those of others. As an adult, you are in charge of managing your own boundaries. It does not follow, however, that others will necessarily respect your boundaries just because you respect theirs. In such cases, you need to know how you will uphold your boundaries and, when necessary, to protect yourself. Remember that not all boundary violations are abusive. For example, if you accidentally jostle someone's arm in a crowd, you are technically violating a boundary, but you are not being abusive.

Types of Boundaries

Boundary/need areas can be divided into two main types: internal and external. These main types can be divided into five smaller groups, as presented below:

Boundaries—limits in relationships. Boundary areas are physical, sexual, emotional, psychological, and spiritual.

Internal Boundaries/Needs

● *Emotional*—This is the ability to differentiate between your feelings and someone elses. You have an inborn need to express yourself, and this includes emotional expression. Emotions provide you with information about yourself in relation to something or someone else. Expressing feelings to yourself or to others is natural. At times, you may need to take a stand and express feelings that are uncomfortable or unpopular. For instance, respectfully expressing anger is not always comfortable, but it is necessary if you are to preserve relationships. Otherwise, anger can become bitterness or resentment, which are very destructive in relationships.

● *Psychological*—This is the ability to know yourself, understand yourself in context, and trust your ability to relate to others based on that knowledge. You are an individual with your own personality. You need to feel okay about your personality and interpersonal style. When you don't like the way you relate to others, you need to be able to make your own choice about changing your style. For example, if you are basically shy, you don't have to pretend not to be or avoid people because you think you will have to fake feelings. On the other hand, you may decide that you don't like being shy and you want to work on that. Psychological boundaries are subtle. Trusting your instincts and listening to your inner thoughts are important. While it is beneficial to be open-minded, you should take care not to dismiss your own positions in the face of a challenge from someone else. You are becoming the expert on yourself.

● *Spiritual*—This is the freedom to choose one's own belief system independent of others. It means the freedom to be your deepest, truest self (spiritual violations include those interactions resulting in self-loathing and unhealthy shame where you feel that you are to blame for interactions you could not have controlled). Spiritual boundaries are about protecting your inner "rightness": rightness with the world around you, yourself, and/or your relationship with a higher power.

External Boundaries/Needs

● *Physical*—This is the freedom to determine under what conditions one will be physical with others without violating their boundaries. Physical boundaries include personal space and belongings. *Physical boundary needs may change several times a day depending on your environment.* For instance, expectations of physical contact at home differ from those at a mall.

● *Sexual*—This is the freedom to determine under what conditions one will be sexual with others without violating others' boundaries. Many survivors don't want to acknowledge their sexuality for various reasons. Some-

Tool: Boundaries

times they can't bear to think about it, or they want to be non-sexual. It is important to face your sexuality since ignoring it can often lead to denial of a significant part of being human. Sexual needs may be expressed in many ways. Sexual needs can be met alone or with another person. Some people express their sexuality by deciding to be celibate or by abstaining from sexual contact with others. Celibacy is not just what's left if you don't have a significant other. It can be a choice that you make for your own well-being. It can be a temporary or a permanent choice (with the option of changing your mind!).

Even if you deny your needs because of past boundary violations, they still exist and will probably affect a lot of your behavior. In other words, ignoring certain needs or certain aspects of yourself won't make your needs go away. You need room to feel and express emotions. You have your own interpersonal style and relate to others accordingly. You are an emotional, psychological, spiritual, physical, and sexual person. Traumatic experiences can influence what you believe about all of these aspects of yourself. Healing involves revisiting these beliefs and challenging them. Healing also involves allowing yourself to feel angry about broken boundaries and the shame that resulted from violations.

Tool: Boundaries

Boundary Worksheet 1

Answering the following will enable you to look at your current boundaries. Think of the changes that you would like to make in how you manage boundaries. For each question, use the boundary types from the previous pages to determine which kind of boundary is at stake. Ideas about which responses show good boundaries are listed at the end.

1. A person you hardly know always greets you with a hug. How do you handle this? (Circle the letter that applies)

A. Hug the person

B. Avoid the person

C. Tell the person you'd rather not hug

D. Put your hand out in hope that he/she takes the hint

This is a _____ boundary.

Would you like to work on a different response? If so, how would you like to respond next time?

_____

_____

Are there other examples of this type of boundary on which you would like to work?

_____

_____

_____

2. A friend of yours tells a lot of racist jokes. You value this friendship so you

A. Laugh even though you don't like it

B. Avoid the person

C. Act like you didn't hear it

D. Tell the person how you feel

This is a _____ boundary.

Would you like to work on a different response? If so, how would you like to respond next time?

_____

_____

Are there other examples of this type of boundary on which you would like to work?

_____

_____

_____

3. Whenever you make mistakes, you tell yourself that you're no good. This thought comes up frequently. You handle it by

A. Saying it over and over in your head

B. Challenging those kinds of messages in your head

C. Trancing out or self-punishing

D. Striving for perfection

This is a _____ boundary.

 Tool: Boundaries

Would you like to work on a different response? If so, how would you like to respond next time?

_____

_____

Are there other examples of this type of boundary on which you would like to work?

_____

_____

4. Whenever you express feelings of anger, your parent tells you that you should really feel guilty because it isn't right to get angry with people who love you. You handle this by

A. Ignoring it   C. Agreeing
B. Reasserting your true feelings   D. "Losing it"

This is a _____ boundary.

Would you like to work on a different response? If so, how would you like to respond next time?

_____

_____

Are there other examples of this type of boundary on which you would like to work?

_____

_____

_____

5. A friend of yours has indicated a sexual interest in you, but you don't feel the same. You handle this by

A. Telling your friend the truth   C. Lying about your sexuality
B. Going along with it for fear of losing   D. Avoiding the issue
the relationship

This is a _____ boundary.

Would you like to work on a different response? If so, how would you like to respond next time?

_____

_____

Are there other examples of this type of boundary on which you would like to work?

_____

_____

_____

6. Your boss at work constantly gives you tasks at the end of the day and expects them to be done before you leave. He does not give you overtime pay, and you have to stay late at least three nights a week. You handle this by

A. Asking for a meeting to discuss this problem C. Not doing the work
B. Doing the work without complaint   D. Quitting

This is a _____ boundary.

Tool: Boundaries

Would you like to work on a different response? If so, how would you like to respond next time?

_____

_____

Are there other examples of this type of boundary on which you would like to work?

_____

_____

Answer key- 1. C   2. D   3. B   4. B   5. A   6. A

7. List some situations in which it is easy for you to justify ignoring or violating your own boundaries.
Example: Self-harm violates physical boundaries but the need for relief can make it seem like a good idea at times. Or, you spend time with people you don't really like because you hate being alone.

_____

_____

_____

_____

_____

_____

8. Where or from whom did you learn that this kind of behavior was okay?

_____

_____

_____

_____

_____

_____

9. What would happen if you began to be more protective of your boundaries? What do you stand to lose? What could you gain?

_____

_____

_____

_____

_____

_____

 *Tool: Boundaries*

Boundary Worksheet 2

1. What boundary areas are most difficult for you to manage? Why?

_____

_____

_____

2. What kinds of boundaries are you more successful at managing? Why?

_____

_____

_____

3. Are there boundaries you are willing to ignore to get your needs met? What are they?

_____

_____

_____

4. What feelings come up when you get your needs met at the expense of your boundaries?

_____

_____

_____

5. What feelings come up when you get your needs met more directly, without sacrificing your boundaries?

_____

_____

_____

6. What do you believe about your right to get your needs met?

_____

_____

_____

Tool: Boundaries

Boundary Worksheet 3

1. Sometimes you can set limits and people will still cross your boundaries. What can you do when this happens? What are you willing to do?

Example: Tell the person how you feel; reduce contact with someone; or only have phone contact.

_____

_____

_____

_____

_____

_____

2. Sometimes others set limits, and you may have a hard time dealing with or accepting those limits. What makes it hard for you to accept reasonable limits?

_____

_____

_____

3. What kinds of feelings do you have when you don't defend or protect your boundaries?

_____

_____

_____

4. What feelings come up when you *do* defend or protect your boundaries?

_____

_____

_____

5. Describe someone you know who has good boundaries. How can you tell that he or she has them?

_____

_____

_____

6. Is this person a good model for showing you ways for managing your boundaries more effectively? If so, list three things this person does that you would like to begin doing.

_____

_____

_____

_____

_____

 Tool: Boundaries

Boundaries Worksheet 4

Building Trust

Building trust is a slow process for trauma survivors. Trust is a two-way street that needs attention and occasional re-pairing. Trust requires faith. Faith requires belief. Belief requires trust. So, in order to build trust, you need a tiny bit of trust to start with. If nothing else, you need to trust in the possibility of trusting. There are a few important ingredients in any trusting or trust-building relationship.

Ingredients:

- Risk
- Reliability
- Consistency
- Honesty
- Forgiveness
- Respect
- Acceptance

1. Are there people in your life who exhibit these characteristics? If so, name them.

_____

_____

_____

2. Which of these characteristics do you think you possess?

_____

_____

_____

3. How do you typically decide if you can trust someone?

_____

_____

_____

4. What happens when someone you trust does something that makes you question his or her trustworthiness?

_____

_____

_____

5. How do you feel when someone says s/he can't trust you?

_____

_____

_____

6. How do you feel about the possibility of repairing broken trust in relationships that are important to you?

_____

_____

_____

Tool: Boundaries

7. What can someone else do to repair broken trust with you?

_____

_____

_____

8. What can you do to repair broken trust with someone else?

_____

_____

_____

9. Are there some situations in which trust cannot be repaired? If so, what situations?

_____

_____

_____

Use the space below, or a separate sheet of paper, to draw a picture of trust.

Tool: Boundaries

Shame

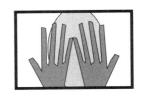

Goal: To develop a clear distinction between healthy and unhealthy guilt and shame.

Idea: Thinking about boundaries may bring to mind situations when your boundaries were abusively violated. One of the most destructive effects of abusive boundary violations is the profound sense of shame that survivors may experience. There is something about sexual abuse in particular that can create a deep and destructive belief within victims that they are bad, to blame for the abuse, or even evil. Shame is a big problem for many survivors, yet who would want to talk about it? Discussing shame increases feelings of exposure and vulnerability. In spite of the discomfort that arises when shame is discussed, survivors need to deal with it in order to separate their identities from their experiences. In other words, many victims of trauma feel that they are defined by their trauma. Their experiences have collapsed on their sense of self and have covered it over with a thick layer that prevents growth and recovery. Dissociation, avoidance, and numbing can actually increase shame-based beliefs by maintaining secrecy and denial.

To really understand shame, it helps to see how it differs from guilt. You also need to separate healthy shame from destructive shame.

Guilt—A feeling arising from having violated your own values or beliefs; includes feelings of remorse, regret, and sorrow; prompts you to make amends, to make up for what you have done; shows up in a good person who has made a mistake or engaged in bad behavior.

Joanne made plans to see a movie with her friend Marie on the same day that she had previously agreed to volunteer at the local soup kitchen. After calling to cancel her plans with Marie, who had been looking forward to the evening, Joanne felt guilty about disappointing her. She called Marie again and invited her to volunteer with her and then go to a movie afterward.

In this example, Joanne feels guilty because she doesn't like to disappoint her friends. However, her obligation to her volunteer work is very important to her. She didn't do anything wrong. She made a mistake and then took steps to make amends.

Healthy Shame—A painful feeling caused by awareness of guilt, shortcoming, or wrongdoing; a sense of dishonor or disgrace; something that brings strong regret or self-blame. Healthy shame arises when our behavior has a much more serious effect than behavior that might only cause guilt

 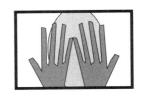

feelings; shows up in a good person who has engaged in bad behavior or disgraced him/herself.

Allen went to a party with friends and had too much to drink. On the way out the door, he stumbled and broke a favorite lamp belonging to the host of the party. He didn't tell anyone what happened and quickly left. Later, he heard about the lamp and his friend's disappointment that no one had admitted to breaking it or offered to have it repaired. Allen felt guilty and ashamed of his behavior that night. He wanted to get the lamp fixed but felt embarrassed about the whole episode. Allen finally called his friend, who was relieved to have the matter cleared up.

In this example, Allen feels guilty about his behavior (getting drunk, breaking the lamp), but he feels ashamed because he was too out of control to take responsibility for his behavior when the incident happened. He also feels ashamed and embarrassed that it has taken him so long to admit his behavior and make amends. He has evaluated himself and has found himself lacking. He resolves to be honest and make those amends. In time, his acute sense of shame will fade, though he may remember the experience with regret for a long time.

Destructive Shame—Negative self-evaluation where there is a sense of self-hatred; feeling bad, worthless, flawed, or unworthy of anything good; includes feelings of exposure and extreme embarrassment; feeling like a bad person who will always do or cause bad things because he/she has a bad, flawed, or destructive nature.

Denise's friend Rachel has just called to tell Denise that she's not a real friend and that Rachel never wants to see her again. Yesterday Rachel had asked Denise for money, and Denise said she couldn't afford to give her any. Denise is on a fixed income and she has to save money in order to get her car repaired. Rachel became angry and told Denise that she was being selfish. Over the past few months, Denise has given Rachel money several times, but has yet to be repaid. Denise believes that friends should help each other out and feels guilty for not giving Rachel her car money. She begins to feel very selfish and wants to take the money to Rachel immediately so she won't be mad. Denise begins thinking that Rachel is right, she's a selfish person and a terrible friend. No matter what she does, she ruins people's lives and hurts everyone. She's never been able to keep a friend no matter how hard she tried. She doesn't deserve friends anyway. If people knew the things she's done, they would run as far from her as they could. Nobody in their right mind would ever want to be her friend. She tells herself that she is a total loser.

In this example, Denise seems to be making a reasonable decision. In fact, her "friend" Rachel appears to be a real user, taking from Denise all of

 Shame

128

the time and expecting Denise to do whatever she wants, whatever the cost. Even though Denise has made a reasonable decision, she is overwhelmed with guilt and shame for being so selfish. Destructive shame (a long-time companion for Denise) has taken over to make her feel responsible for Rachel's anger and rejection. It has blinded her to the reality that Rachel uses her and isn't a real friend at all.

Where Does Destructive Shame Come From?

Destructive shame arises in abuse survivors for several reasons, including 1) the belief that the abuse is their fault, 2) the feeling of being worthless or no good, and 3) the humiliation associated with having been abused to begin with. Traumatic and prolonged shame experiences, especially those occurring early in life, can lead to ongoing negative self-talk and destructive shame.

In the context of early and prolonged traumatic shame experiences, there is usually an extreme difference in power between the people involved. In other words, the shame experience involves (at least) two people with very different degrees of power in the relationship (i.e., caregiver and child). The person with the most power (caregiver) is responsible for managing appropriate boundaries and looking after the general welfare of the person with the least power (the child). However, if a shameful act (abuse) takes place, and the person with the power does not take responsibility for it, where does the shame go? The disowned shame falls on the weaker person in the interaction. The more powerful person may blame the less powerful person, thus reinforcing the shame experience and deepening the sense of responsibility for the act. The more powerful person may even concoct lies to support his/her own denial and disownership of responsibility. The more vulnerable person may even believe the lies and internalize them as part of his/her reality. The weaker person may conclude *It is my fault.*

Examples of shaming statements include:

- "Now look what you made me do."
- "Don't make me get angry."
- "You can't do anything right."
- "How could you be so stupid?"

The process of healing involves teasing apart the various threads of guilt, shame, blame, power, control, and responsibility that weave together in a traumatic experience. However, not all experiences need to be evaluated. Survivors need to discover the patterns of shame disownership that shaped their experiences of traumatic events and their beliefs about them.

Anger

There is a relationship between shame and anger, as well as between shame and violence. We are rarely aware of this relationship. Anger is first and foremost an energy emotion. It mobilizes forces inside of you that call you to action. Anger makes you want to *do* something. What you do with it can hurt or heal, or can bring about positive change or destruction. Your responses to anger can lead to hope or despair.

Anger and Despair—There is a type of hopeless, helpless anger that cannot be expressed if you are threatened with harm. This form of anger can become inextricably entwined with despair. It is a protective defense against endangering one's self by expressing anger in threatening circumstances, and it is the sort of anger that depletes energy. Anger linked to despair can grow to depression or to a feeling of impotent rage. It is hungry for expression but finds no avenue of release. It is, therefore, seen as useless and as something that must not be felt. Present-day anger can tap into past anger and despair and can confuse you about the present. You may have a very hard time with angry feelings because they tap into strong feelings of hopelessness. It helps to assess yourself in the moment to figure out how much of the anger comes from the current situation, and how much of it is "old."

Someone who is dependent on another for survival must maintain some kind of truce with that person. If the one you have to depend on is dangerous and controlling, it is not at all adaptive for you to show opposition. Angry feelings might prompt opposition and endanger you further. However, if the anger becomes embedded in despair and is then turned inward, such a process becomes a survival adaptation. Many abuse survivors are terrified of feeling anger because they fear that they will become violent. Some avoid dealing with anger because it is so connected to helplessness and despair. The terror around expressing anger can be paralyzing. People who cope by using substances or who get involved with other addictive behavior (self-harm) typically do so at this point. The fear and perceived threat about anger can almost be described as an emotional flashback: an intrusive recollection of feelings connected to traumatic experiences. But another kind of anger can be more present-focused, and it is a form of anger connected with hope.

Anger and Hope—There is a kind of anger that recognizes the way things are (vs. the way they could be) and motivates a person to act. This

Anger

anger creates motivating energy and allows a person to see possibilities and move toward them. This anger enables the person to mobilize resources within and without.

For example, Dr. Martin Luther King, Jr. was incredibly angry about the lack of civil justice in American society. However, he could see the possibility of change. He had hope for society and worked tirelessly toward a dream he believed in with all his heart.

People who are truly in touch with their anger can use it as a source of energy and power to achieve their goals. Being aware of anger reduces the likelihood that you will lose control. Unacknowledged anger will invariably rule you. It will show up in areas of your life and come out in unclear ways at inappropriate times or when you don't really mean it.

Under *normal* circumstances (in situations that don't involve trauma or abuse), **empathy** is the best defense against overwhelming anger. If you can see a situation from someone else's point of view, you may be able to tone down your anger. That is the key to dealing with anger in healthier relationships. Understanding your reactions and yourself is the beginning. The next step involves working to understand the other person involved. Keep in mind that empathy is helpful in non-traumatic interactions. Use the following pages to work on a better understanding of your own anger reactions.

Empathy—the ability to put one's self into the psychological frame of reference or point of view of another.

Anger Worksheet 1

1. I am afraid of my own anger because _____
_____
_____

2. I can't deal with other people's anger because _____
_____
_____

3. I get rid of my anger by _____
_____
_____

4. When someone else is angry with me I have to _____
_____
_____

5. My anger feels like _____
_____
_____

6. If I drew my anger it would look like _____
_____
_____

Read over your responses. Do you notice anything about the thoughts and beliefs that show up in your responses?
_____
_____

Do any of your answers reflect the things you learned about anger when you were young?
_____
_____

Think of one person in your life who expresses anger safely and in healthy ways. List all of the ways this person expresses anger.
_____
_____

List three healthy ways you've been able to express anger or have seen others able to express it.
_____
_____
_____

 Anger

Anger Worksheet 2

Healthy expression of anger starts with owning anger as *your* feeling that tells you something about *yourself* in relationship to someone or something else.

For example, If Jane becomes angry because her friend is 45 minutes late for a lunch date, what does that tell Jane about herself? It may tell her that 1) she believes people should be on time for appointments, 2) she believes that it is inconsiderate to be so late, 3) when people are very late, she fears for their safety, or 4) she believes that a person who is 45 minutes late should at least call the person who is waiting. Jane's anger says more about her than it does about her friend. Why? Because, until she speaks to her friend, Jane does not have enough information to know why her friend is late. Thus, all of the assumptions Jane makes have more to do with her than with her friend.

What kinds of situations prompt anger in you? What does your anger tell you about yourself?

List some situations in which you usually become angry. Then, document what you are learning about yourself in relation to your anger.

Situation:_____

_____

What it tells you about yourself: _____

_____

_____

Situation:_____

_____

What it tells you about yourself: _____

_____

_____

Situation:_____

_____

_____

What it tells you about yourself: _____

_____

_____

Situation:_____

_____

_____

What it tells you about yourself: _____

_____

_____

Anger

Situation:_____

_____

_____

What it tells you about yourself: _____

_____

_____

_____

_____

Situation:_____

_____

_____

What it tells you about yourself: _____

_____

_____

_____

_____

Situation:_____

_____

_____

What it tells you about yourself: _____

_____

_____

_____

_____

Situation:_____

_____

_____

What it tells you about yourself: _____

_____

_____

_____

_____

Anger

Anger Worksheet 3

In this worksheet, you will find some ideas about managing anger. Think about someone you know who manages anger effectively, and add ideas of your own.

Things You Can Do:

exercise	clean house	work in the garden	take time out to cool off
walk the dog	use deep breathing	use a sense of humor	call a friend and vent
write an anger letter	get rid of junk		
(don't mail it!)			

_____

_____

_____

Things You Can Say:

To yourself:

"I am so angry."

"Hello my little anger." (Zen Buddhist trick)

"My anger feels like _____."

"This anger leads me to think about _____."

_____

_____

_____

_____

_____

_____

To the person you are angry with:

"I feel angry with you for _____."

"I feel angry and disappointed about _____."

"I feel angry and hurt by _____."

"I feel too angry to talk right now."

_____

_____

_____

_____

_____

_____

Anger can be closely tied to emotional pain. Don't worry or be surprised if you find sadness, sorrow, grief, hurt, or similar feelings underneath your anger. Crying can help defuse anger.

Anger

Anger Worksheet 4

Use the space below to hold any angry feelings that may have come up while you worked on these pages. Write or draw using two or three colors. Avoid drawing scary images and using negative self-talk.

Example—You could write using the format, "I'm angry about" . . . or "I'm angry with you because". . . .

_____

_____

_____

_____

_____

_____

Use the box to draw your feelings.

 Anger

Connecting thoughts with experiences, feelings, impulses, and behaviors can be a challenge for survivors. Working to re-establish connections that have been ignored or shut down can be even more difficult. But it is these connections that enable survivors to feel more in control and less vulnerable on a daily basis.

It is all very nice to learn a number of techniques and ideas about managing difficulties differently, but what happens when you are put to the test? The next section will help you to use what you have learned so far. It will help you to put tools together in a way that can help you not only manage the day-to-day struggles, but the crises too.

Putting Tools Together

Putting Tools Together

Up to this point, this workbook has focused on specific skills and techniques to help you with regulating thoughts, feelings, and impulses as well to assists you in dealing with traumatic stress reactions. Now it's time to look at ways of packaging or linking those skills in order to develop a healthier coping strategy. Putting the skills together to address different difficulties is part of learning new coping habits. The ways that you cope do become habitual, and as with any habit, you have to work hard and pay attention in order to change unhelpful habits of coping. It is useful to take the whole arsenal of self-regulation skills you have learned and use as many as possible during a difficult situation. This increases the likelihood that some method will prove helpful. However, there are several very structured ways of applying coping skills in order to get started.

Please remember that it is up to *you* to decide which interventions work best for you. While it is helpful to practice most of them, not all interventions apply to all people. This workbook offers guidelines and suggestions that have worked for thousands of people, but each of those people customized the interventions to meet his or her needs. You are the authority on *you*. Listen to your instincts and make use of the interventions that seem best suited to you.

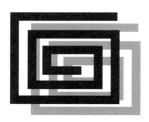

Tools for Regulation of Thoughts

Intrusive thoughts are a major part of posttraumatic and dissociative experiences. These thoughts may be related to past trauma, fear of future trauma, or old messages of self-doubt and criticism. People learn these ways of thinking at a very young age. As you grow up, others around you teach you their thoughts, opinions, and views of the world through words or actions. In abusive environments, these thoughts and beliefs are most often geared toward controlling others. In other words, *the thoughts may not be based on the truth but rather on control and manipulation.* Children who are abused often have had to take on such thoughts and beliefs in order to survive. As an adult today, you have an opportunity to look at those thoughts and beliefs and decide whether to challenge or change them.

Managing intrusive posttraumatic and dissociative thoughts is important because in your thoughts you will find the keys to your feelings and behavior. It is very important to learn the differences and the relationships between thoughts, feelings, and behaviors if you are to make changes in them.

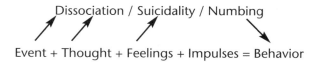

Dissociation / Suicidality / Numbing

Event + Thought + Feelings + Impulses = Behavior

This diagram shows that thoughts, feelings, and behaviors are related. Events happen in your life. Some events are big like birthdays and weddings, and some are small like getting bills or not getting an expected phone call, but all events have an effect. When an event, thought, or feeling is seen as overwhelming, you may find yourself zoning out (dissociating), numbing, or focusing on thoughts of self-harm, aggression, or suicide. Dissociation and suicidality can take attention away from thoughts and feelings about events in your life. This can seem like a good solution when you are distressed, but when you think about it, the relief doesn't usually last too long and it causes a whole lot of other problems. Usually dissociation, avoidance, and suicidality do very little to help a person cope with problems and result in more problems, like impulsivity and dangerous behavior.

Events can be just as bad as we think they are *or* the *thoughts* or *judgments* that we have about them may cause us more distress than the actual events.

For example, if a car goes speeding down the road after cutting you off, you might think the driver is an insensitive jerk. However, if you know there's a

child in the car in need of immediate medical attention, you might think the speeding is justified.

In both cases, the event is the same. Someone is speeding away after cutting you off. Your thoughts determine how you will feel based on whether you *think* the event is justified. Often, it is difficult to know enough of the story to decide whether something is okay, so you make assumptions based on your experiences. If your experiences have been traumatic, your basic assumptions may insist that most events are negative and pose a threat, even when they don't! These kinds of assumptions can be a one-way ticket to a flashback because they may vividly and intrusively remind you of traumatic past events. That is not to say that some events aren't every bit as bad as you think they are, but survivors need to be attentive to their traumatic *interpretations* of potentially mild or neutral events.

Regulation of Thoughts Worksheet 1

Intrusive thoughts can surface seemingly without rhyme or reason. These thoughts can be critical, traumatic, anxiety-provoking, distracting, or just plain bothersome! Intrusive thoughts are usually negative and can lead to other problems like poor concentration, irritability, intrusive images, flashbacks, and impulsive behaviors. Often, you may want to simply ignore the thoughts, but this doesn't always work. They can come back more powerfully than before. Below you will find a list of some common intrusive thoughts. Add some of your own to the list.

1. Things will never get better.
2. I can't do anything right.
3. Feelings are dangerous.
4. If people really knew me, they'd hate me.
5. Nowhere is safe.
6. No one is safe.
7. I can't change.
8. Something bad is going to happen.
9. Shut up! Don't talk!
10. I am bad.
11. _____
12. _____
13. _____
14. _____
15. _____
16. _____
17. _____
18. _____
19. _____
20. _____

What kinds of feelings typically go along with these thoughts?

_____
_____
_____
_____

What kinds of impulses typically go with those feelings? In other words, when you feel that way, what do you think about doing?

_____
_____
_____
_____

 Tools for Regulation of Thoughts

Thinking the same thoughts you learned from people who may have been trying to control you may be a way of controlling yourself. In other words, if one of your thoughts is "I am just crazy," and your caregivers or perpetrators used to tell you this to keep you from talking, why might you tell yourself the same thing? Thinking that you're crazy may *protect* you from having to deal with the truth of others' actions. It can be a defense against reality that allows you to preserve the dream/wish that you have about those relationships.

Some people with DID hear intrusive thoughts from other parts of themselves in ways that serve the same purpose. One part may constantly tell the rest to "Shut up" in an effort to keep from getting oneself into trouble with outside people. This would be protective in an abusive environment, but is probably interfering with your life today. Those parts need to be taught that you are an adult and aren't in danger the way you used to be. Those parts need to be taught grounding.

Are there any common themes or beliefs associated with your intrusive thoughts? If so, what are they?

_____

_____

_____

Can you think of how you came to believe these things?

_____

_____

_____

How might these beliefs be protective today?

_____

_____

_____

How do these beliefs interfere with your life today?

_____

_____

_____

In the words of one survivior . . .

"Negative thoughts about yourself take away responsibility for your actions. You don't need to take care of something bad. It can be destroyed . . . [this] leads to a vicious cycle of nothingness."—S.M (Consumer/Survivor/Advocate)

Regulation of Thoughts Worksheet 2

Having identified some of your intrusive thoughts, it may be helpful to develop some challenges to those thoughts. Challenges can help you to consider a new way of thinking. They can provide you with options so that you can choose how you will focus your thoughts and ideas about events in your life. Let's create some challenges to the intrusive thoughts listed on page 144.

A challenge thought has two requirements: it has to be neutral (nonjudgmental) and it has to be true.

Example:

Intrusive Thoughts	*Challenges*
1. I am selfish.	1. It is important to take care of myself.
2. I am incompetent.	2. I am proud of my ability to . . .
3. I have to get away.	3. I am an adult, I have other resources, I can . . .

Things will never get better.
Challenge_____

_____

I can't do anything right.
Challenge_____

_____

Feelings are dangerous.
Challenge_____

_____

Nowhere is safe.
Challenge_____

_____

No one is safe.
Challenge_____

_____

I can't change.
Challenge_____

_____

Something bad is going to happen.
Challenge_____

_____

 Tools for Regulation of Thoughts

Shut up! Don't talk!
Challenge_____

_____

I am bad.
Challenge_____

_____

If people really knew me, they'd hate me.

Challenge_____

_____

Add some of your own thoughts and challenges.

Thought _____
Challenge_____

_____

Thought_____
Challenge_____

_____

Thought_____
Challenge_____

_____

Thought_____
Challenge_____

_____

Thought_____
Challenge_____

_____

Thought_____
Challenge_____

_____

Thought_____
Challenge_____

_____

Now that you have looked at some of the sources of intrusive thoughts and have discovered why you may be struggling with them, it helps to develop a plan you can use to manage when you begin to have intrusive thoughts in your daily life. The diagram below shows how events, thoughts, feelings, and impulses can lead to behavior. If the event is troubling, and the thoughts are scary or negative, the feelings are likely to be upsetting and can lead to problematic impulses and behaviors.

EVENT + THOUGHT + FEELING + IMPULSE = BEHAVIOR

The first opportunity to change things comes right after an event has occurred. Right after something happens, you have thoughts or judgments about the incident that has happened. The best thing to do when you feel upset or thrown for a loop is to *check it out*. See if things have happened the way you are thinking they have happened. The process of checking things out is called a "reality check."

A reality check involves taking a step back from intense feelings to mentally review or reconsider the event. Slow things down. Take a breath. You may have to put feelings aside or turn them down (see the chapter on Imagery) in order to do a reality check. You may have to ask others their opinions. The more grounded you are, the more effective your reality check will be. Use grounding techniques to help you to focus on the present. The important thing to remember is that neglecting to do a reality check may lead to misinterpretation of what has happened, or, worse, to flashbacks.

Tools for Regulation of Thoughts

Managing the Event

EVENT +	THOUGHT +	FEELING +	IMPULSE	= BEHAVIOR
-grounding -reality check				

After the event:

1. Use the grounding techniques discussed earlier in this book. Remaining present-focused is the key to managing flashbacks.

2. Do a reality check. Did the happen the way you think it happened? If so, is it as bad as it seems? Along with the reality check, make sure you are connected and grounded in the present.

EVENT +	THOUGHT +	FEELING +	IMPULSE	= BEHAVIOR
-grounding	-grounding			
-reality check	-reality check			
	- notice thoughts			
	-challenge the thoughts			
	-journal			
	-talk			
	-use imagery			

Address your thoughts

1. Notice the thoughts you are having, and observe them. For example, say to yourself, "I'm aware that I am thinking that this is the worst possible thing that could happen." Name the thoughts: "That is a catastrophic thought"; "That is a fearful thought"; "That is an impulsive thought."

2. Challenge the thought using self-talk: "This is not necessarily a disaster. I don't know the whole story. I don't have to figure this out right now. I don't have to act now. I don't have to pretend this doesn't bother me. I can get some help with this." "I can set time aside to work on this, and get back to the person involved later."

3. Use your journal to write down your thoughts and the challenges you have for them. Make sure your challenges are nonjudgmental and true.

4. Talk to yourself in your mind; tell yourself about new ways of handling the thoughts; remind yourself that you are an adult; and say who your helpers are today.

Use imagery. Imagine a dial in your head, and turn the thoughts down. Dim them to a lesser intensity. Remember the section on imagery, and use the techniques from it to reduce the intensity of your intrusive thoughts. Help other parts of yourself (if you have DID) to express feelings more directly rather than through having upsetting thoughts. This requires discipline and commitment, but the result is worth it!

Tools for Regulation of Thoughts

Remember these processes:

Experience: Notice that you are struggling with intrusive thoughts. Name them to reduce their power over you. Realize that they are only thoughts that don't necessarily represent reality.

Express: Say something to yourself or to a trusted friend or therapist; use self-talk to express what you are thinking. Use self-talk to challenge those thoughts.

Contain: Put the thoughts aside for a while. Jot them down in a journal and leave them alone for a time. Use imagery to visualize a stop sign or to picture the thoughts being written down in a book that you can close.

Retrieve: Return to the thoughts later when you are feeling less vulnerable. Check them out. Do they still make sense to you? Are they as strong as they were? Are you able to distinguish thoughts that are reality from those that are wishes or fears?

Thoughts lead to actions; we do what we think about. That is why it is better to "Think of what you want, rather than what you fear." (*The Silver Boat,* by Ann Adams).

Regulation of Feelings

The management of intense feelings will build on what you have learned about managing intrusive thoughts. Many people with histories of trauma believe that the goal related to managing feelings is to "get them out" so they won't be bothered by them anymore. However, the more useful goal related to feelings is to *get them in*.

Feelings are a natural part of being human. It is *unnatural* to feel numb or overwhelmed all of the time. Not only are feelings natural, but they are important because they tell you how you are doing in relationship to someone or something else. Feelings direct your attention and are protective. When children have feelings, they usually express them immediately. For a child, feeling and expressing are virtually the same thing.

Often, survivors find feelings to be threatening. This may be the case because feelings can be scary or painful. Being in touch with feelings during painful experiences can seem intolerable. If traumatic experiences were an everyday part of your childhood, you may have learned that expressing feelings was dangerous. You may have had to learn not to have feelings. Maybe you learned ways to make them go away or perhaps you learned how to go away yourself. In any case, making feelings go away may have been the only way for you to manage.

Today, things can be different. First of all, you are an adult. Who are the allies in your life? Perhaps you have supporters whom you didn't have as a child (maybe a therapist). You have learned some other adult ways of coping, although you may still use dissociation, avoidance, or numbing as your main means of coping. The truth of the matter is, not having access to feelings may get you into trouble these days. It is important to understand how that can happen.

Consider the following questions.

1. When you are numb, are you more likely to get involved in unhealthy or dangerous relationships?

2. When you are going away inside, are you more likely to have flashbacks or hurt yourself?

3. When you feel overwhelmed and you numb out, do your feelings come back stronger later?

4. Do you end up having overwhelming feelings about the smallest things?

If you answered "Yes" to any of these questions, it might make sense to try some new ways of managing feelings.

Suggestion: right now, go back to the toolbox section, and read through the chapters on introduction to self-regulation, grounding, imagery, and journal writing. *Really* read over those sections. They are very important when it comes to working with feelings. You will need to refer to them over and over.

Do you remember the recipe for self-regulation?

1. Experience
2. Express
3. Contain
4. Retrieve

Experience what is going on inside. Notice the way you feel. Get in touch with it. You may ask, "How do I get in touch with my feelings?" Stop doing whatever it is you do to make feelings go away! For example, you may have to stop getting rid of feelings by overeating or undereating, drinking or using drugs, or by overspending or behaving in reckless ways. If you stop these behaviors, you will have feelings; don't worry. When you begin to feel them, don't cut them off in a panic. Feelings naturally come and go in waves. They get stronger and weaker as you feel them. You have to risk sitting with feelings to notice this. Don't make them stronger. Just notice them. Observe them.

Express your feelings. Say something to yourself or to someone else about the way you feel. Make a remark like, "I notice I'm feeling sad and angry at the same time, and I notice that this scares me." Draw how you are feeling (not what you feel like doing); write about it in your journal. Create an image that matches your feeling. Maybe your sadness and anger feel like a powerful rainstorm. Imagine that they *are* a rainstorm. Imagine the intensity increasing and decreasing just like it does with a storm. After the storm, there may be evidence of what happened, but the intensity has passed and there may even be a calm.

Contain the part of your feelings that is too much. You can learn to get used to your feelings by spending time with smaller amounts of feeling. Frequently, an intense feeling will attach from the past. When this happens, you have to learn the difference between the feelings about the past and the ones that are about the present. For instance, you may feel disappointed in a friend who cancels out on a lunch date with you. You may feel sad, angry, and disappointed. The problem is that bigger feelings of anger, sadness, and disappointment from the past may come up and bring even bigger feelings of rage, grief, and abandonment, creating a sense of betrayal. Is it reasonable to say that your friend who couldn't make it to lunch betrayed you? It probably isn't reasonable. It is very important to separate past feelings from the present situation so that you can deal with your present feelings in the moment.

Retrieve or revisit part of the feeling later. What did it feel like? Was it an old familiar feeling in a new situation? Did it improve or reduce your ability to keep track of the present? What does that feeling mean to you? Allow yourself to re-experience a *small* part of the feeling. You don't have to get it back full force. It's better to focus on a small piece of it. For example, if you felt angry earlier today, and it built into rage and feelings of helplessness which led to your feeling trapped and threatened, try to focus on the anger and what led up to it while you postpone talking about, writing, or drawing about the other more overwhelming feelings.

EVENT +	THOUGHT +	FEELING +	IMPULSE	= BEHAVIOR
-grounding -reality check	-grounding -reality check -notice thoughts -challenge thoughts -journal -talk -use imagery	-grounding -reality check -notice feelings -talk -journal -artwork -use imagery		

To review, feelings are largely determined by your thoughts. So when you are having trouble with intense feelings, you will also have to address your thoughts. Your thoughts may be based on a recent event, so you need to review what has been going on in your life lately. Or, you may be experiencing intrusive thoughts from the past. Whatever you may be thinking about will affect your feelings. Using all of these techniques will help you to make sense of your feelings, making it easier for you to manage them more effectively.

In order to address feelings and work on them, you have to notice them. You need to allow yourself to become aware of feelings without pushing them away. Only then can you begin your interventions.

Address feelings:

1. Stop what you are doing, and use grounding techniques to get focused. (Review the chapter on grounding.) What techniques help you to get grounded? How will you remember to use them? Can you keep a small notebook or index card with you to remind you of what works? Name five things you see in the present, five things you hear, five things you feel physically, and so on.

2. Do a reality check. Ask yourself questions such as the following: "Is this as terrible as it feels? Is it likely that these big feelings are intruding from

Regulation of Feelings

the past?" Make sure you're grounded. Are you confusing this situation with one from the past? Are you thinking old thoughts? Are you getting trapped in old ways of thinking and feeling? Review your resources (grounding, journal, imagery, etc.).

3. Talk to yourself inside and talk to reliable outside people. Remind yourself that relationships can be different in the present. Use self-talk to work on identifying your feelings. Are you mad, sad, or glad? Keep it simple at first. Use the list of Feeling Words in the back of this book (Appendix A) to identify feelings. Your thoughts and impulses can also be clues to your feelings.

4. Use your journal to help you figure out the difference between the past and the present. Write about how your feelings are affecting you. What reactions are coming up related to your feelings? Are your feelings based on the current situation or are they based on past experiences and expectations? Don't forget to look at your thoughts and consider how they are contributing to your feelings. You can create a table in your journal that will help you see the difference between the past and the present.

Draw this chart in your journal to show how a situation is similar to and/or different from the past.

Same as past	Different from past
Example: Feeling angry & hopeless	I am an adult now
Someone is minimizing my needs	I might be able to get this need met differently

Make a pie chart in your journal that shows how much feeling is about today and how much is about the past.

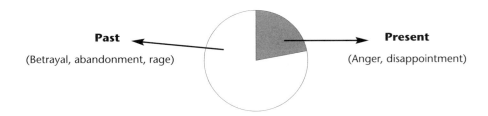

Past
(Betrayal, abandonment, rage)

Present
(Anger, disappointment)

5. Use artwork to draw a picture of how you are feeling. Your feelings may look like many different colors swirling together; or they might be more like a volcano. Creating a picture of your feelings can help you to use imagery to manage them.

6. Use imagery to increase (if numb) or decrease (if overwhelmed) the intensity of your feelings. Start by checking your internal gauge to see how intense things are. Next, use your internal regulator to turn things to a more tolerable level. Visualize the whole process. Then contain the overwhelming piece of your feelings in a safe holding place. Remember to keep a small part of the feeling to work on getting used to your emotions. Talk with someone, draw, or write about the small piece.

7. Contain the part that is about the past, and put it aside in your mind. You will come back to it later.

    A. Draw a type of container that will hold those feelings. Visualize them going inside of the container. Draw your container in the box below.

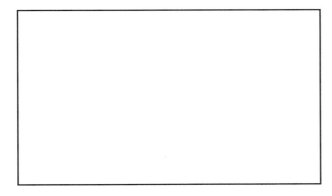

    B. Contain feelings by drawing them in your art book, by writing in your journal, by using images of containers that you have practiced using, or by talking about them.

Feelings Worksheet 1

Feelings are like oxygen. You need them to live, but too much or too little over long periods of time makes life very difficult. Without access to feelings, you are very likely to find yourself in sticky situations or unhealthy relationships. Sometimes you will not even know how you got where you are. The key is to make it safe to have all of your feelings, to get used to them so they don't scare you. Containing the overwhelming parts of your feelings will help you to be more effective when it comes to managing the feelings you are having about the present. It is up to you to think of a container image that will hold your overwhelming feelings. Here are some images that have worked for others. Draw or cut and paste some of your own images in the boxes below:

1. Hot air balloon

2. Safe with or without a time lock

3. Box

4. Dam with spillway

5. Genie bottle/lamp

6. Vacuum cleaner

 Regulation of Feelings

What are some images you like?

7.

8.

9.

10.

11.

12.

Feelings Worksheet 2

Don't forget that self-regulation of feelings requires that you retrieve what you have stored. That is, you have to revisit feelings in small doses and work on them so that they won't keep building up. If you don't intend to retrieve what is stored, what you are doing is just fancy "stuffing" and it won't help much.

The best time to retrieve the feelings you stored is when you are feeling calmer and stronger. Another good time might be during a therapy session.

The following is an example of what can happen if you don't work on managing thoughts, feelings, impulses and behaviors.

EVENT +	THOUGHT +	FEELING +	IMPULSE	= BEHAVIOR
Friend can't go to lunch	"She doesn't care. I can't rely on anyone"	Sad, lonely, angry, disappointed	Go to a bar, get drunk, pick up somebody	Go to a bar, get drunk

What are your coping activities? Use the space below to show how this situation could be managed differently. Again, remember to apply the techniques that you have practiced and that are most helpful to you.

EVENT +	THOUGHT +	FEELING +	IMPULSE	= BEHAVIOR

Regulation of Feelings

Feelings Worksheet 3

Think of a recent *non-traumatic* event that was troubling to you. Write down what happened. Add the interventions you would use for the event, thoughts, and feelings next time. Be specific. If you would use grounding, write in the specific technique that you would use.

EVENT (What happened?)

_____

_____

_____

What could you do for a reality check, for grounding?

_____

_____

_____

THOUGHT (What did you think about the event after it happened?)

_____

_____

_____

What techniques would help you manage these thoughts in the future?

_____

_____

_____

FEELING (What feelings came up?)

_____

_____

_____

What techniques would help you manage these feelings in the future?

_____

_____

_____

IMPULSES (What impulses did you have?)

_____

_____

_____

Regulation of Feelings

BEHAVIOR (What did you ultimately do?)

_____

_____

_____

Do you think the outcome might have been different had you known techniques to manage thoughts and feelings?

_____

1. How could the outcome be different if you paid attention to thoughts and feelings as opposed to avoiding them?

_____

_____

_____

2. How could staying in touch with thoughts and feelings benefit you in the long run?

_____

_____

_____

3. What would you have to give up to change the way you manage feelings?

_____

_____

_____

4. How committed are you to making changes in how you manage feelings? (Circle one)

      10%   20%   30%   40%   50%   60%   70%   80%   90%   100%

 Regulation of Feelings

Feelings Worksheet 4

   It is useful to map out some past situations during which you may have ignored or numbed feelings. This activity will enable you to review the historical/typical outcomes. Go over these past situations and identify what techniques might work in the future. This will help you plan for the next time you have intense feelings. Make choices that are effective rather than satisfying. Go with what will work for you in the long run. Remember that feelings are a natural and necessary part of being human, and disowning or denying them leads to impulsivity and unsafe behavior. Today, in the present, paying attention to feelings can lead to a safer, more satisfying life. In fact, you will need to have access to your feelings in order to monitor how your relationships are going. You cannot avoid "bad" or uncomfortable feelings without losing "good" or happy feelings. It's up to you to decide if the tradeoff is worth it.

   Think of another past situation in which you shut out feelings and behaved impulsively. Trace the events, thoughts, feelings and impulses that led to your behaviors.

EVENT (What happened?)

_____

_____

THOUGHT (What did you think about it?)

_____

_____

FEELING (What feelings came up?)

_____

_____

IMPULSES (What impulses did you have?)

_____

_____

BEHAVIOR (What did you ultimately do?)

_____

_____

Is there a specific point at which you typically shut down, shut feelings out, numb out, or dissociate? If so, when does it occur?_____

_____

How does shutting down help/harm you?_____

_____

_____

Regulation of Feelings

Regulation of Impulses

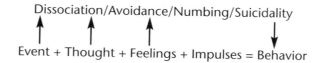

Dissociation/Avoidance/Numbing/Suicidality

Event + Thought + Feelings + Impulses = Behavior

Dissociation, avoidance, and numbing are processes that distance you from your own thoughts, feelings, and impulses. These processes create the impression that impulses come on with no warning at all. Feeling suicidal can work in the same way to change your focus and reduce your ability to notice thoughts and emotions. The reduction of awareness of feelings can seem protective but is actually very dangerous. Dissociation, avoidance, numbing, and suicidality can create a detour that seems protective and reassuring but in reality will leave you vulnerable. If you intend to gain better control of your impulsive behavior, it is essential to work on grounding to combat dissociation, avoidance, and numbing. With a reduction in avoidance behaviors, you will be more likely to see the cues and clues that tell you when you are truly in danger or when your level of impulsivity is increasing.

An **impulse** is an action urge. It can begin as an idea or it can come on quickly with energy that prompts you to act. The key to managing impulses is to wait out the urge without acting on it. This is not to say that you "white knuckle it." You have to do *something* with the energy. It's *what* you do that counts. Consider the origins and functions of impulsivity.

Being repeatedly exposed to a traumatic environment can teach you several things about impulses. You may learn that 1) other people are impulsive and don't seem to resist their impulses, 2) acting on impulses can relieve the constant thoughts of the impulse, 3) acting on impulses can relieve tension inside, and 4) acting on impulses can distract you from threatening feelings. While these things may have been true in past environments, they probably are not true about everyone or every situation. You may have learned other things about impulses that are less obvious, such as: 1) acting on impulses can make a situation worse; 2) the process of acting on impulses can get out of control; 3) acting on impulses does nothing to help you cope more effectively in the long run; 4) acting on impulses can be dangerous; and 5) acting on impulses can become addictive since the relief doesn't last and the impulses become more frequent.

In other words, you may have learned early in life that impulsive behavior is acceptable. Also, you probably found impulsive behavior helpful when there was no support or help available. However, today, in the present, impulsive behavior usually has more negative consequences and can lead to self-harm, suicide, homicide, stealing, recklessness, and other behaviors that are guaranteed to get negative reactions from others and make you feel worse about yourself.

Impulsive behavior involves a tradeoff. Will you trade safety for temporary relief? If you think about it, that's exactly what abusers do. Abusers ignore the safety needs of the victim in order to relieve their own feelings or satisfy their own desires at the expense of the victim. Rationalizing unsafe, aggressive, or abusive behavior is very dangerous. Beware of that kind of thinking in your own life.

Impulsivity Worksheet 1

Write your initial reactions to the question, "Will you trade safety for relief?"

_____

_____

_____

Are your reactions based on fear, reality, or a wish that you have?_____

Below you will find a list of impulses commonly experienced by people with histories of childhood trauma. Circle the impulses that you experience currently. Add any that aren't listed.

Self-harm   Aggression toward others   Suicidality   Overeating   Undereating

Drinking   Misusing medication   Using drugs   Reckless driving   Overspending

Risky behavior (Examples: on the streets at 4 a.m.; prostitution; seeking out abusive people)

_____

_____

_____

How are you typically feeling before the impulses get strong? What emotions usually lead to impulsivity for you? (_Examples:_ sadness, loneliness, anger, etc.)

_____

_____

_____

What kinds of thoughts typically lead to impulsivity for you? (_Examples:_ "It'll never get better," "I can't stand this," "I don't care anymore.")

_____

_____

_____

What kinds of events have led to impulsivity in the past? (_Examples:_ getting fired/hired, receiving a phone call from a past perpetrator)

_____

_____

_____

Regulation of Impulses

Impulsivity Worksheet 2

How does impulsive behavior help you? (*Examples:* self-harm, overspending, etc. might temporarily make bad feelings go away.)

_____

_____

_____

What are some of the negative effects of impulsive behavior? (*Examples:* Loss of friends, money, etc.)

_____

_____

_____

What are some of the conflicts you have about stopping impulsive behavior? (*Examples:* "I struggle with being willing to have emotions instead of making them go away.")

_____

_____

_____

There can be no arguing that impulsive behavior can relieve internal pressure in the short term. You have to decide whether the consequences are worth it. You can choose to use self-regulation skills to manage impulses instead. These skills will enable you to reduce impulsivity and manage thoughts and feelings in a more lasting way. Over time, your dangerous impulses will decrease in intensity, in just the way that smokers who have quit feel less desire to smoke. It is natural to have cravings or impulses from time to time, but acting on them will no longer be an option.

The challenge is to be honest with yourself when you are impulsive. *I am choosing this impulse instead of self-regulation. I want a quick fix; the consequences don't matter. The effect it may have on others doesn't matter. Nothing matters more than getting immediate relief.* Now be honest—isn't that the same reasoning abusers probably used to justify their behavior? Sometimes being honest will help you to stay safe. It will help you to make the healthy choice.

If you feel ready to do so, identify a few impulses you would like to begin fighting.

1._____

2._____

3._____

Acting on impulses hides the feelings that actually fuel the impulses. The key to managing impulses is to keep from acting on them and then deal with the feelings that led up to them. Avoidance will not work forever.

Impulsivity Worksheet 3

EVENT +	THOUGHT +	FEELING +	IMPULSE	= BEHAVIOR

-grounding
-reality check
	-grounding
	-reality check
	-notice thoughts
	-challenge
	   thoughts
	-journal
	-talk
	-use imagery
		-grounding
		-reality check
		-notice feelings
		-talk
		-journal
		-artwork
		-use imagery
			-grounding
			-substitute action
			-exercise
			-imagery
			-journal
			-artwork
			-call therapist
			-call hotline
			-call friend or
			   sponsor
			-call 911
			use PRN
			   medication as
			   prescribed
				New Behavior

Remember the activities you looked at in the previous chapters on self-regulation. You may want to review them. You have learned activities for each point in the sequence, and you know what you can do to manage your stress responses at each intervention point. Now develop a plan to intervene with your impulses.

Address your impulses:

1. Impulses are action urges. They come upon you with energy and make you want to do something. Sometimes you will need to do a safe alternative activity to help use or reduce the energy that comes with an impulse. Make sure that the substitute activity is *nothing* like the impulse! If you have an impulse to punch walls, don't substitute by punching a pillow. Sometimes doing a similar substitute will lead to the impulsive behavior. And it doesn't make sense to substitute violence for violence.

2. Use healthy, non-compulsive exercises to release the energy associated with an impulse. Go for a walk. Work in the yard. Call a friend to go out with you. Whatever you do, make sure you can do it safely.

3. Use imagery while you are engaging in a substitute activity. Imagine that the impulse is floating up into the sky in a giant balloon. If you use your energy to clean your house, imagine that your vacuum is sucking up

Regulation of Impulses

all of the unhealthy impulses and containing them in the vacuum bag. Visualize a regulator that controls levels of impulsivity, and turn it down. Imagine that your impulsivity can be released through a steam vent.

4. You can use your journal to document your impulses and the feelings that may be fueling them. Ask yourself, *what would I be thinking about if I weren't focused on my impulses? What healthy thing can I do instead?*

5. Use artwork to find out what feelings are fueling the impulse. Keep art supplies on hand. Crayons, markers, oil pastels, or chalk pastels can be used to show how feelings look inside. You might draw a volcano or swirls of color showing confusion. Artwork is very helpful for self-expression. Avoid drawing unsafe impulses or violent pictures. They can be re-traumatizing or may lead you closer to impulsive behavior.

6. If the impulse is serious and is a potential threat to you or someone else, you need to be willing to call your therapist (if you have one), a hotline, or 911. You need to evaluate for yourself what it means to involve the police in your area. Some regions have well-trained officers who are very helpful in a crisis, some don't. *Safely* wait for help, and accept the help that is offered. Calling for help can be a challenge, but it is an important act. While you are waiting for the return call, be sure to use the interventions you have learned (grounding, imagery journal writing, self-regulation, safety plan, etc.).

7. You may have medication that you can take to reduce your impulsivity. Check with your doctor about this. **It is NEVER okay to misuse your prescription medication.** That is unsafe and represents a serious breach of trust between you and your doctor. Use your medication as prescribed. If you have PRN medication (medication prescribed to be used as needed according to symptoms and recommended dosage), use it *before* you are completely overwhelmed. Then, use the techniques taught in this book. A combination of medication and therapeutic techniques will have a greater benefit than the medication alone. Work hard to choose healthy alternatives. Don't rely on the medication alone.

It is essential to make a list of safe things you can do when you are impulsive. Keep the list in a place that you can get to it if you need it. Laminate it so it will last. Practice becoming aware of how you get drawn into old patterns of thinking and feeling that have historically led to dangerousness and/or impulsivity.

Impulsivity Worksheet 4

Sometimes it helps to work backwards when tracing patterns of impulsivity. Use the image below to describe a time when you acted impulsively.

EVENT +	THOUGHT +	FEELING +	IMPULSE	= BEHAVIOR

1. What behavior did you engage in?

_____

_____

2. What impulses did you experience before you did the behavior? What did you think about doing, and what did you visualize?

_____

_____

_____

3. What emotions were you feeling before you became impulsive?

_____

_____

4. What thoughts were going through your head that may have led to the feelings? What had you been thinking about?

_____

_____

_____

5. Had something happened recently to prompt those thoughts? Had there been a recent event that disrupted you? If so, what was it?

_____

_____

_____

6. How were your thoughts and feelings related to your impulses and behavior?

_____

_____

_____

7. Did your behavior resolve anything? If so, what did it resolve?

_____

_____

_____

8. Did your behavior make anything worse? If so, what did it make worse?

_____

_____

_____

9. Was the consequence worth the payoff?_____

If so, why?_____

_____

_____

_____

If not, why not?_____

_____

_____

_____

10. How would you deal with it differently next time? How would you remind yourself of your options?

_____

_____

_____

_____

_____

_____

Regulation of Impulses

Identifying events, thoughts, and feelings that prompt impulses and behavior can help you to: 1) manage impulses more effectively, 2) defuse triggers and intense feelings, and 3) increase your ability to feel safe in the world. Naturally, the sooner you intervene with posttraumatic and dissociative experiences, the less likely you are to become impulsive. And, the sooner you pay attention to thoughts and feelings, the less likely they are to build up and lead to impulses.

You probably learned somewhere from someone that acting on feelings is the only way to deal with them. The problem is, acting impulsively always leads to more feelings. Usually these feelings are worse than the ones you started with, like guilt and shame. This is a vicious, addictive cycle that creates the need for more acting out to get rid of the new feelings. It takes a lot of work and dedication to stop this cycle. As an adult, it's up to you to decide whether you will make changes in your behavior. You can decide when and how to make those changes. Remember that change is very difficult, but choosing change that benefits you because *you* want to is an experience of freedom and recovery.

Regulation of Sensory Experiences

No handbook on managing difficulties associated with PTSD and dissociation would be complete if it did not address the various disruptions that people may experience through one or more of their five senses at any given time. These stress responses are intrusive, and they make it very hard to maintain contact with reality. If left unmanaged, these difficulties can lead to dangerous behaviors.

Where do these experiences come from? Keep in mind that traumatic experiences are stored in your brain differently from non-traumatic experiences. All or parts of these experiences can come back to you as intrusive recollections. Therefore, a traumatic event can sometimes come back as something you are seeing in your mind's eye or as a visual hallucination. Traumatic hallucinations differ from psychotic hallucinations and can be managed through the techniques taught in this handbook. In the same way that you might see things that aren't really there in the present, you might hear, taste, smell, or feel things that aren't there. This chapter will focus on how to prevent these experiences and how to deal with them when they occur.

The most crucial factor in managing intrusive sensory experiences is knowing the difference between present reality and recollections of past experiences. Intrusive stress responses can arise very quickly. The goal of management is to learn skills that will give you the opportunity to notice when these experiences are coming and to reduce their intensity.

On the next few pages you will find tables describing posttraumatic intrusive experiences and useful interventions. You may need to review the Toolbox sections on grounding, imagery, journal writing, and relaxation again in order to make use of the techniques in this section.

Posttraumatic Response	Prevention	Management
Intrusive visual images (Seeing traumatic or scary things that aren't really there in the present)	Grounding Reality checks Feelings check in	Grounding Reality checks Name stress response Imagery Journal writing Self talk PRN Call for help
Intrusive sounds (hearing things in your head or outside of yourself that aren't coming from outside sources, but are coming from your mind)	Grounding Reality checks Feelings check in Self talk	Grounding Reality checks Name stress response Imagery Journal writing Self talk PRN Call for help
Intrusive tastes and smells	Grounding Reality checks Feelings check in Regular Journal writing	Grounding Reality checks Name stress response Imagery Journal writing Self talk PRN Substitution Flooding (as a technique) Call for help Post-hypnotic suggestions
Intrusive physical sensations like "body memories" and other sensations	Grounding Reality checks Feelings check in Regular Journal writing	Grounding Reality checks Name stress response Imagery Healing light imagery Healing pool or waterfall imagery Shrink & Roll Journal writing Self talk PRN Call for help

Regulation of Sensory Experiences

Grounding—When you are experiencing intrusive stress responses, you must focus on becoming connected to the present in order to be aware that you are experiencing an intrusive recollection rather than a "real-time" trauma. If you can acknowledge the experience as a stress response, you will be more grounded. Use your five senses to promote grounding, as is discussed on page 32.

Reality check—Reality checks to combat intrusive stress responses should focus on separating the past from the present and distinguishing between traumatic stress responses and present reality. For example, you may need to accept that while the pain or discomfort is real, the cause may be due not to current trauma but rather to an intrusive recollection of past trauma. *However,* if you are currently involved in abusive relationships where you are being harmed, you need to understand that you will be more likely to experience intrusive stress responses in addition to the current abuse. If that is the case, you may need to seek professional help to deal with your current situation.

Feelings check-in—Be sure to check in with yourself about your feelings several times each day. Perhaps even share them with a trusted friend. Frequently, fearful feelings can lead to intrusive stress responses. Since fear is probably closely associated with past traumatic events, feeling intense fear in the present can "trigger" intrusive experiences. Use the techniques you have learned to decrease the intensity of feelings.

Name the stress response—If you can identify your intrusive sensations as stress responses, they will be less likely to lead to flashbacks. When these responses arise, you really have two choices: either 1) the experience is a real traumatic event that is happening now, or 2) it is a stress response. If you decide that it is real (but in reality it is a stress response), then you are more likely to dissociate, numb out, avoid, lose time, and possibly have an extremely re-traumatizing flashback. However, if you correctly recognize the experience as a stress response, you won't be helpless to control it. You can use the interventions taught in this book.

PRN—PRN is a Latin abbreviation that means "as needed." Some people have medication prescribed that may be taken "as needed" when trauma responses are getting bad. The key is to take the medication when you recognize the signs of a bad spell, and then also use other techniques like imagery to help the medication work. Imagine the medication moving through your body, reducing anxiety, soothing you, and helping you to stay grounded.

Regulation of Sensory Experiences

Imagery—Use imagery as discussed earlier and try the following techniques.

Healing light imagery—The healing light could be whatever you want. Try using sunlight. Imagine the warm sun overhead, bathing you with gentle light, warming you down from the top of your head. As the light travels through your head, neck, and body all the way to your feet, it pushes out any tension, fear, anxiety, body pain, or stress responses until you are filled with the light and feeling better. Some people like to use healing colors and change whatever color they have inside (like orange) to another, more soothing color (blue). The technique works the same way as the healing light imagery, or you may want to imagine inhaling the soothing color and exhaling the painful color.

Healing pool or waterfall imagery—This is similar to the healing light, except that you use the image of a gentle pool or waterfall that washes away anything you need to get rid of (not feelings!). You can step into a private pool or step under a protective waterfall that gently washes away tension, stress, and pain.

Shrink and Roll—This technique works very well on body pain or other intrusive physical sensations. First, visualize the uncomfortable feeling resting in a place that you can tolerate, like your stomach or head. Then imagine that the feeling (physical, not emotional) is a lead ball that begins to shrink and move toward your arm. As it gets to your shoulder, it gets even smaller, becoming the size of a golf ball. It grows smaller again as it passes your elbow, and smaller still, as it gets to your wrist. Now it's the size of a pea. As it moves toward your index finger, it shrinks to the size of a tiny dot and you can roll it out of your finger and put it into an imaginary container. You can do this with headaches too—just roll them out through your earlobe.

Journal writing—Writing can help you to figure out the difference between the past and the present. Write about whether the current experience is an old feeling in a new situation or a new feeling altogether. Use your journal after the stress response has faded, to record the experience and trace what may have led up to it. When you are struggling with stress response reactions *do not* use your journal to *graphically* describe the traumatic experience, or you may become overwhelmed again.

Self talk—Talk inside and outside. Use self talk to work on identifying reality. For example, ask yourself, "Is it more likely that this is happening now or that it is a symptom of posttraumatic stress or dissociation?" Remind yourself of the resources you can access: hotlines, friends, family, or a therapist. If you have written these things down ahead of time, it will be eas-

Regulation of Sensory Experiences

ier to make use of them. Keep a resource card on you at all times. Include numbers for hotlines, friends, your sponsor, your therapist, and other supportive people.

Substitution—If you are having trouble dealing with intrusive tastes or smells, try substituting another taste or smell. Chew gum or suck on a mint; drink ice water or coffee. Use potpourri, scented candles, or hand lotion to create a soothing smell. Remember to use this technique *with* the others you have learned.

Flooding (this technique should be distinguished from the *symptom* of flooding in which you become overwhelmed by emotions)—If you are somewhere and a particular real-time smell is triggering you, take three long, slow, deep breaths through your nose. This will fill up or flood your sense of smell so that you won't smell it as strongly. Flooding is a natural process that happens all of the time when you no longer notice a smell because your nose is flooded. Think about times when you may have noticed a particular smell right away, but after a while, you didn't seem to notice it anymore. That is flooding, and you can make it work for you. Of course, if you smell smoke or some other dangerous smell, act accordingly to ensure your safety.

Post-Hypnotic Suggestion—If certain tastes and smells come up for you a lot (from your head, not from the environment), you may need to use a different taste/smell to "trigger" grounding and relaxation. To do this, you and your therapist must work together. First, choose a safe, soothing taste/smell. Let's say you chose lemons. You would work in therapy to practice grounding and relaxation as you think of lemons or eat lemon candy. After awhile, just the thought of lemons will help you feel calmer and more grounded. Then use that technique whenever the intrusive tastes and smells come up.

Call for help—Sometimes you may need extra help to fight your post-traumatic and dissociative experiences. You need to know whom and when to call. For instance, you don't always have to call a therapist if it isn't an emergency. You can call a supportive friend who can remind you of what is helpful or help you turn your mind toward more soothing thoughts. By the same token, you can call a friend when your situation is really serious, but you need to be careful not to "dump" on your friends. Talk with friends ahead of time to set boundaries around the kind of help they can offer in a crisis. If you think you are really in danger of self-harm or suicide, call your therapist, a hotline, or 911, and wait for help (remember the chapter on safety).

Peer Support Networks

There is a peer support movement afoot in the survivor community. This movement is oriented toward providing peer support, based on a wellness model. In other words, it provides support based on what people can do for each other, and how they can help one another on a day-to-day basis rather than through using a symptom- or problem-focused model. This is part of an overall shift away from the medical model of treatment to a trauma/adaptation model.

Peer support is a system of helping and receiving help based on respect, shared responsibility, and a shared definition of what's helpful without making assumptions about others. Being able to spend time with others who have "been there" is very important. It reduces shame and feelings of alienation while it increases feelings of understanding and being understood without having to rehash personal history over and over. Peer support is a movement towards independence *and* community.

Peer support can provide a number of the key ingredients for recovery, such as the following:

- belief in one's self,
- having others believe in you, and
- taking control of your life.

Empowerment and wellness are encouraged in the community of peers through a sense of connectedness and the existence of healing relationships. It offers survivors an opportunity to try things out in a safe community. At the same time, it is a "real" community, not artificially created, but some little piece of the world where people are free to experience being who they are. And survivors are so much more than the sum of their pain and traumas. Peer support based on wellness allows survivors to explore new identities as people, beyond survival.

Peer support groups help people to

- Practice clear boundaries
- Practice and become comfortable with decision-making power
- Learn about choices
- Learn to identify and clearly state needs
- Own the belief that you can make a difference
- Own the belief in a possibility of change and growth
- Be hopeful

- Feel a part of a community
- Organize according to what the group thinks is important
- Build a social network

Where do peer support groups come from?

You! Check the resource page in the back of this book for peer support contacts. Why not start a peer support group? There is a lot of help available and plenty of information on what has worked for others.

Conclusion

If you have reached this page, I hope it means you have made your way through this handbook and have found it helpful. The material you have studied may be helping you already, or you may be having trouble with part or all of it. That's normal. There are a few common complaints/concerns that should be addressed in case you are having trouble.

1. No, you don't have to be able to do these skills perfectly.

2. No, you don't have to be able to use everything immediately, although some techniques may provide you with immediate relief. These skills take a lot of time and practice. There is no "overnight" success. Some techniques will work more quickly than others.

3. Yes, there is hope for recovery. It takes time and work, but there are many people who have spent the time and done the work and are living life in a way they never thought they could.

4. No, not all of the techniques work all of the time, but if you use as many techniques as possible to manage your posttraumatic and dissociative experiences, you are more likely to get relief than if you use only one or two. Practice mixing and matching until you find the ones that work best together and in certain situations.

Finally, if you have other thoughts, suggestions, complaints or feedback, please feel free to send them to me. I welcome your comments about this book. Feedback about these materials can be directed to me at:

> Elizabeth G. Vermilyea
> c/o The Sidran Traumatic Stress Foundation
> 200 East Joppa Rd., Suite 207
> Baltimore, MD 21286
> elizabeth@sidran.org

I will consider your feedback carefully.
One last note. If you have finished this workbook from start to finish,

Start again!

Glossary

Affect—feeling and expression of emotion or mood.

Attachment—the state of developing and maintaining a healthy relationship between parent or other caregiver, and child; the relationship is characterized by a sense of security, emotional attunement, and regulation of physiological functioning such that the developing child becomes able to self-regulate over time; see bonding.

Attunement—an emotional connection between two people characterized by a sense of mutual understanding.

Behavior—physical actions or responses.

Bonding—developing a stable and supportive relationship with a primary caregiver; see attachment.

Boundaries—limits in relationships. Boundary areas are physical, sexual, emotional, psychological, and spiritual.

Conscious—present awareness.

Container—a holding environment or storage for intrusive or overwhelming thoughts, feelings, impulses, or stress responses.

Containment—the process of intentionally postponing dealing with upsetting thoughts, feelings or impulses, implies a willingness to revisit the problem later when one is feeling more stable.

Dissociation—a separation of the normally integrated or connected functions of identity, perception, personality, and memory.

Empathy—the ability to put one's self into the psychological frame of reference or point of view of another.

Experience—the process of personally observing, encountering, or undergoing something.

Express—to acknowledge and communicate something internally to yourself and/or externally to others.

Feeling/Emotion—a mood state that focuses your attention, provokes physical and physiological responses, and involves the expenditure of physical, mental, and behavioral energy.

Fight or Flight Response—a physiological response to perceived danger that activates the mind and body to defend or to flee.

Flashback—an intrusive and vivid recollection of a traumatic experience, at times so realistic that it becomes difficult to tell whether the traumatic experience is happening in the moment or not, may involve one or more of the five senses (sight, taste, smell, touch, or hearing).

Flooding (symptom)—the process of becoming overwhelmed by intrusive emotions, sensory experiences, or intense re-living experiences; commonly associated with posttraumatic stress disorder.

Gauge—an image used to measure intensity of thoughts, feelings, or impulses.

Grounding—present-focused awareness, achieving a sense of connectedness to yourself and your environment.

Guilt—a feeling of remorse or regret from having made a mistake or caused someone else pain or discomfort; promotes a desire to make amends or change behavior for the better.

Imagery—using your imagination to manage stress responses and feelings.

Impulse—an action urge, an urge to do something.

Journal Writing—the process of using structured exercises to write about thoughts, feelings, and stress responses in an effort to increase self-awareness and decrease symptomatology.

Manipulative—using indirect methods to get a need met or to get what one desires.

Mental—relating to the total emotional and intellectual response of a person to the environment, pertaining to the mind.

Mindfulness—paying attention to oneself, noticing what is going on inside.

Nurturance—promotion of development, teaching, training.

Power—a sense of connectedness to your own ability to manage and direct your life (not to be confused with power over others).

Pre-conscious—accessible memory.

Posttraumatic stress condition—troubling or disruptive thoughts, feelings or impulses resulting from one or more traumatic experiences.

Posttraumatic stress disorder (PTSD)—a disorder that can develop when a person is exposed to traumatic events beyond their ability to cope; symptoms include intrusive experiences, avoidance experiences, and increased nervous system arousal (heightened nervous system activity).

PRN Medication—medication prescribed "as needed," to be used at the discretion of the patient within certain guidelines.

Reality check—a technique that helps you to become aware of the true state of affairs in a particular experience.

Regulator—an imagery technique used to help you control the intensity of thoughts, feeling states or intrusive experiences.

Relaxation—tension- or stress-reduction.

Re-traumatizing—re-enacting or reinforcing a traumatic experience or belief.

Resistance—in therapeutic terms, a natural tendency or instinctive opposition to change or exposure of thing that you don't like about yourself.

Retrieval—the process of "revisiting" a portion of your feelings, thoughts, or traumatic material that has been contained.

Sadism (Sadistic)—pleasure derived from inflicting pain or cruelty on someone else.

Safe—the condition of being reasonably free from harm or immediate threat of harm regarding your five boundary areas.

Safe Places—real or imaginary places that you can visualize in order to feel safer, calmer, or to take a break from intense thoughts, feelings, or impulses.

Self-esteem—a sense of your own worth or value.

Self-regulation—the process of consciously managing different internal states by 1) experiencing them as they come up, 2) expressing what you are experiencing, 3) consciously postponing dealing with traumatic material or overwhelming aspects of feelings, and 4) retrieving part of what you have contained when you are better able to manage it.

Sensation—information from experiences that involve one or more of your five senses.

Shame—a feeling of wrongness about the self, feeling as if one is a mistake or is flawed in some basic way.

Stressor—a particular event or experience that requires the use of coping skills; traumatic stressors are particular traumatic events or experiences that overwhelm adaptive coping skills.

Thoughts—inner mental processes that describe how you gather, store, retrieve, and use knowledge about yourself and the world.

Trance—a state of highly focused awareness often to the extent that awareness of the self or environment is shut out.

Traumatic Stress Response—the emotional, physiological, and psychological reaction to a traumatic event.

Unconscious—inaccessible memory.

Appendix

Feeling Words

Adoration	Crushed	Humiliated	Reluctant
Affection	Curious	Hurt	Remorseful
Afraid	Dazed	Incompetent	Resentful
Aggravated	Defeated	Indifferent	Sad
Agitated	Delighted	Infatuated	Satisfied
Agonized	Desire	Insecure	Scared
Alienated	Despairing	Insulted	Secure
Amazed	Destructive	Interested	Sentimental
Amused	Determined	Isolated	Shocked
Angry	Disgust	Jealous	Shy
Annoyed	Displeased	Joyful	Skeptical
Anxious	Distressed	Jumpy	Sorrowful
Apprehensive	Doubtful	Kindness	Spiteful
Arousal	Euphoric	Loathful	Surprised
Ashamed	Excited	Lonely	Suspicious
Attraction	Exhilarated	Longing	Tenderness
Bitter	Fidgety	Love	Tense
Blue	Fondness	Mad	Terrified
Bored	Fragile	Miserable	Threatened
Brave	Frightened	Misunderstood	Thrilled
Caring	Furious	Mortified	Triumphant
Cautious	Glad	Nervous	Trusting
Charmed	Glum	Overwhelmed	Uneasy
Cheerful	Grieving	Panicked	Unhappy
Compassion	Grouchy	Paralyzed	Unsure
Competent	Guilty	Passion	Vengeful
Concerned	Happy	Pleased	Warm
Confident	Hateful	Powerful	Weary
Contemptuous	Helpless	Rageful	Worried
Content	Hopeful	Regretful	
Contrite	Hopeless	Rejected	
Cruel	Horrified	Relieved	

Resources

Peer Support

Susan Mockus

    c/o The Sidran Traumatic Stress Foundation

    200 East Joppa Rd., Suite 207

    Towson, MD 21256

    RIGHTYES@aol.com

Support for victims of crime.

National Organization for Victim Assistance (NOVA)

    1757 Park Road NW

    Washington DC 20010-2101

    phone 202-232-6682; fax 202-462-2255

    e-mail: nova@try-nova.org

    internet: www.try-nova.org

Coalition of sexual assault and rape crisis centers. Information and referral.

National Coalition Against Sexual Assault (NCASA)

    125 N. Enola Drive

    Enola PA 17025

    717-728-9764

RAINN (Rape, Abuse, & Incest National Network)

    635-B Pennsylvania Ave. SE

    Washington DC 20003

    24-hour free hotline: 800-656-HOPE (4673), ext. 1

    online counseling: http://rapecrisis.txcyber.com

    RAINN website: www.rainn.org

    fax 202-544-3556

    e-mail: RAINNmail@aol.com

National Organization on Male Sexual Victimization (NOMSV)

    PO Box 20782

    West Palm Beach FL 33416

    800-738-4181

    website: www.nomsv.org

References/Reading List

Adams, K. (1998). *The Way of the Journal.* Sidran Foundation and Press, Lutherville, Maryland.

Allen, J. (1999). *Coping With Trauma.* American Psychiatric Press, Inc. Washington D.C.

Berliner, L. & Elliott, D. (1996). *Sexual Abuse of Children.* In *The APSAC Handbook on Child Maltreatment.* Sage, Thousand Oaks, California.

Bowlby, J. (1988). *A Secure Base.* Basic Books, New York.

Bremner, J. & Marmar, C., Eds. (1998). *Trauma, Memory, and Dissociation.* American Psychiatric Press, Inc., Washington D.C.

Davies, J. & Frawley, G. (1994). *Treating the Adult Survivor of Childhood Sexual Abuse.* Basic Books, New York.

DeAngelis, T. (1999). *Trauma at an Early Age Inhibits Ability to Bond.* APA Monitor Online.

Diagnostic and Statistical Manual of Mental Disorders. 4th Ed. (1994). American Psychiatric Association, Washington, D.C.

Gainer, M. & Torem, M. (1994). Clinical corner: Sleep and dissociation—New findings. *ISSD News,* August.

Herman, J. (1992). *Trauma and Recovery.* Basic Books, New York.

Karen, R. (1992). "Shame." *The Atlantic Monthly,* 429–449.

Lew, M. (1988). *Victims No Longer.* Harper & Row, New York.

Lewis, H.B. (1971). *Shame and Guilt in Neurosis.* International University Press, New York.

Linehan, M. (1993). *Cognitive-Behavioral Treatment of Borderline Personality Disorder.* Guilford Press, New York.

Lynd, H.M. (1958). *On Shame and the Search for Identity.* Harcourt, Brace and Company, New York.

McCann, I. & Pearlman, L. (1990). *Psychological Trauma and the Adult Survivor.* Brunner/Mazel, Inc, New York.

Morrison, A.P. (1989). *Shame: The Underside of Narcissism.* Analytic Press, London.

Paris, J., Ed. (1993). *Borderline Personality Disorder: Etiology and Treatment.* American Psychiatric Press, Inc., Washington, D.C.

Pfeffer, C. (1996). *Severe Stress and Mental Disturbance in Children.* American Psychiatric Press, Washington, D.C.

Saakvitne, K., Gamble, S., Pearlman, L., & Lev, B. (2000). *Risking Connection.* Sidran Foundation and Press, Lutherville, Maryland.

Sands, S. (1994). "What is dissociated?" *Dissociation*, Vol. VII, No. 3, pp. 145–151.

Silberg, J., Ed. (1996). *The Dissociative Child.* Sidran Foundation and Press, Lutherville, Maryland.

van der Kolk, B., McFarlane, A. & Weisaeth, L., Eds. (1996). *Traumatic Stress.* Guilford Press, Inc. New York.

van der Kolk, B. (1987). *Psychological Trauma.* American Psychiatric Press, Inc., Washington, D.C.

van der Kolk, B. (1997). "The Psychobiology of Posttraumatic Stress Disorder." *Journal of Clinical Psychiatry,* 1997; 58 (suppl 9), pp. 16–23.

Wiesel, E. (1990). "Out of Despair." *American Journal of Psychoanalysis,* Vol. 50, No. 2, pp. 97–108.

Yehuda, R., Ed. (1999). *Risk Factors for Posttraumatic Stress Disorder.* American Psychiatric Press, Inc., Washington, D.C.

Zanarini, M.C. (1997). *Role of Sexual Abuse in the Etiology of Borderline Personality Disorder.* American Psychiatric Press, Inc., Washington D.C.

About the SIDRAN INSTITUTE

The Sidran Institute, a leader in traumatic stress education and advocacy, is a nationally focused nonprofit organization devoted to helping people understand, manage, and treat traumatic stress. Our education and advocacy promotes greater understanding of:

- The early recognition and treatment of trauma-related stress in children;
- The understanding of trauma and its long-term effect on adults;
- The strategies leading to greatest success in self-help recovery for trauma survivors;
- The clinical methods and practices leading to greatest success in aiding trauma victims;
- The development of public policy initiatives that are responsive to the needs of adult and child survivors of traumatic events.

To further this mission, Sidran operates the following programs:

The Sidran Institute Press publishes books and educational materials on traumatic stress and dissociative conditions. Recently published examples are *Risking Connection: A Training Curriculum for Working with Survivors of Childhood Trauma* (for service providers, both professional and paraprofessional); *Risking Connection in Faith Communities: A Training Curriculum for Faith Leaders Supporting Trauma Survivors; Restoring Hope and Trust: An Illustrated Guide to Mastering Trauma;* and *Ethics in Victim Services.*

Sidran Training and Consultation Services provide conference speakers, pre-programmed and custom workshops, consultation, and technical assistance on all aspects of traumatic stress including:

- **Agency Training** on trauma-related topics. Our training has been delivered to a wide variety of providers working with traumatized populations, such as:

  - Mental Health
  - Substance Abuse
  - Corrections
  - Parole and Probation
  - Domestic Violence
  - Child Abuse

  - Clergy
  - Developmental Disabilities
  - Education
  - Youth Services
  - Residential Services
  - and more.

  We will be glad to customize presentations for the specific needs of your agency.

- **Public Education and Consultation** to organizations, associations, and government on a variety of trauma topics and public education strategies.

- **Survivor Education** programming including how to start and maintain effective peer support groups, community networking for trauma support, successful selection of therapists, coping skills, and healing skills.

The Sidran Bookshelf on Trauma and Dissociation is an annotated mail order and web catalog of the best in clinical, educational, and survivor-supportive literature on post-traumatic stress–related topics.

The Sidran Help Desk – drawing from Sidran's extensive database and library – provides trauma resources and referrals at no cost to callers from around the English-speaking world.

For more information on any of these programs and projects, please contact us:

Sidran Institute
200 East Joppa Road, Suite 207, Baltimore, MD 21286
Phone: 410-825-8888 ▪ Fax: 410-337-0747
E-mail: sidran@sidran.org ▪ Website: **www.sidran.org**

EDUCATION • PUBLICATIONS • RESOURCES